The
Meditation
Experience

The Meditation Experience

Your complete meditation workshop in a book

Madonna Gauding

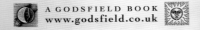
A GODSFIELD BOOK
www.godsfield.co.uk

An Hachette UK Company
www.hachette.co.uk

First published in Great Britain in 2010 by
Godsfield, a division of Octopus Publishing Group Ltd
Endeavour House
189 Shaftesbury Avenue
London WC2H 8JY
www.octopusbooksusa.com

Distributed in the U.S. and Canada by Octopus Books USA:
c/o Hachette Book Group
237 Park Avenue
New York, NY 10017

ISBN 978-1-841-81394-3

Printed and bound in China

2 4 6 8 10 9 7 5 3 1

Note

It is advisable to check with your doctor before embarking on any exercise
program. The exercises in this book should not be considered a replacement for
professional medical treatment; a physician should be consulted in all matters
relating to health and particularly in respect of pregnancy and any symptoms that
may require diagnosis or medical attention. While the advice and information in this
book is believed to be accurate, neither the author nor the publisher can accept any
legal responsibility for any injury sustained while following the exercises.

Yoga, tai chi, and chi kung can be practiced by people of all ages and states of
fitness; always consult a doctor, however, if you are pregnant or have a health
condition. The meditation and visualization exercises included in this book are
designed for relaxation and for developing self-awareness. However, anyone who has
emotional or mental problems, or who has had problems of this nature in the past,
should seek professional medical advice before attempting any of these exercises.
The author and the publisher accept no responsibility for any harm caused by or to
anyone as a result of the misuse of these exercises.

CONTENTS

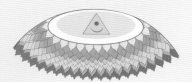

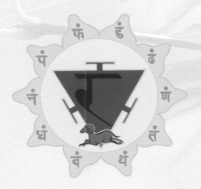

Introduction

This book presents a broad range of meditation techniques for you to sample from around the world. I introduce you to Buddhist, Hindu, Christian, Sufi, Jewish, and other meditative traditions, and expose you to the richness of these practices and their potential for enhancing everyday life. The guided meditations in the book and on the interactive CD will deepen your meditation practice by helping you pay attention to the subtleties of the various feelings and mind states available to you within the meditative experience. It is exactly like attending a workshop to explore how meditation can heal and transform your life. However, instead of condensing the instruction into a weekend, you can take your time and go at your own pace.

This book is both for absolute beginners who know nothing about meditation and those who have some introduction to the subject and would like to enhance their practice. No matter who you are, I encourage you to approach the instruction provided here in a spirit of joyful exploration and with an attitude of kindness and compassion toward yourself. If you find that you don't get on with a particular meditation exercise or find it too difficult, move on to the next one, but leave yourself the option to come back later and give it another try. If you find that you really love a particular meditation practice and begin to incorporate it into your daily life, you can look forward to continued benefits that only deepen over time.

The journey begins

Your meditation journey begins with concentrative meditation. After learning to quiet your mind with this technique, you will move on to explore the content of your thoughts on a deeper level. You will experience how various states of consciousness feel and how they can help heal the body and deepen spiritual understanding. Mindfulness is not only about paying attention to your mind, but witnessing your body and the world around you, too. Most of us are used to living with physical tension, which makes it more difficult to focus on the whole body. Mindfulness meditation will help you begin to feel the energy in

your body and the subtleties of its expression. As you progress, you will next learn to work with sound and image, bringing a new depth and richness to your practice. Lastly, we will explore meditations for developing compassion and loving-kindness.

Although meditation has its source in ancient spiritual practices, you do not have to subscribe to the various beliefs of those traditions in order to benefit. You can practice meditation for whatever reason motivates you—for relaxation, healing, or for personal and spiritual growth. Or you can simply try the exercises in this book with an open heart and mind and see what happens. Meditation is always a journey not a destination. Every person is unique and, over time, if you practice consistently, you will forge your own practice that suits your unique life and goals.

We all bring our personal expectations, past histories, and emotional, energetic, and physical blocks to meditation. We bring our hopes and fears, perhaps that meditation will "fix" us or make

us whole. We bring our health and ailments, and our need for love, compassion, and personal fulfillment. We may long for a stronger spiritual life that shows us the deeper meaning in everyday living. Where you start your meditation is exactly where you are right now. And wherever you are is just fine. I encourage you to experience the practice of meditation and open yourself to its potential for healing and transformation.

How to use the book and CD

This book is divided into sections specially designed to lead you step-by-step into a deeper understanding of meditation. In the first part of each section you will find information about and explanations of the meditation exercises that follow. Each section, each chapter, and each exercise builds on the previous one, so I recommend that you work through them at your own pace in the order presented.

It would be helpful for you first to read through the entire book so you have an overview of how it unfolds. Then begin with the meditations for calming the mind in section 2 (starting on page 49). These will form the bedrock of your practice. Finally, work with a specific meditation for as little or as long as you like. Take your time to explore each form of meditation to see whether it appeals to you.

Using the CD

The accompanying CD offers music tracks as well as guided instruction for some of the meditations. The meditation instructions tell you when to use the CD and will guide you to a specific track. All you need to do is follow the instructions you hear. If you need extra time to practice each stage of a meditation, simply pause the CD and move on when you are ready. Or, if you prefer, you can record your own instructions. You will find the scripts at the back of the book (see pages 242–249).

Any form of daily meditation will bring many benefits to your body, mind, and soul over time. My fondest wish is that this deeper exploration of meditation will help you to develop a daily meditation practice that will sustain you in your daily life.

Recording your experiences

Following each meditation exercise you will find journal pages on which to record your thoughts and experiences. Writing down your insight as you further your practice will help you get the most out of the book. Remember to record the date and time of day.

Some people find it easier to meditate in the morning. Some close the door to their office and meditate during their lunch hour at work, and others prefer meditating in the evening before bed. You may also find that certain meditation practices work better for you at a particular time of day. Noting the time of each practice will give you information about what works best for you for each type of meditation.

It is best if you record your experiences immediately after a meditation session. Record the first thought that comes to mind and try not to censure or edit yourself in any way. Your first thought is usually your best and most accurate one. Remember to note any body sensations you experience during an exercise—such as a change in your breathing and heart rate—and whether you were uncomfortable in any way. Record any experience of tension or relaxation, too, along with any emotions and thoughts that arose during your meditation.

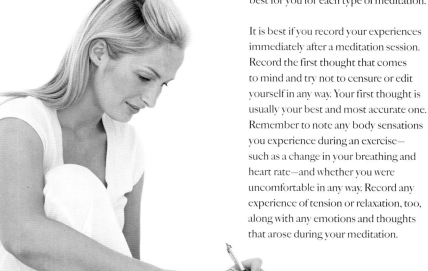

Insightful questions

The journal pages include questions to help you better focus on your experience of a particular meditation. These can be helpful when you come back to a particular meditation. You may also want to briefly check in with yourself before a meditation exercise so that you can note in the journal pages any difference in how you feel after the meditation.

Recording your experiences in the journal pages will help you to remember that meditation is not only a journey, but *your* unique journey. You may feel positive after a meditation, you may feel nothing, or you may even feel negativity or frustration. The main thing to bring to any meditation practice is an attitude of openness and loving-kindness toward yourself that will help you to stop negative self-judgment.

Visual aids to meditation

Throughout the book you will find color photographs and illustrations that will show you the most popular sitting poses for meditation, including the correct use of cushions and mats, as well as giving advice on good posture and breathing essentials. There are also illustrations of common mudras, or hand gestures, used in meditation. These gestures symbolize a deity or a quality that you wish to cultivate, such as wisdom or compassion. Learning mudras and incorporating them into your practice can help make your meditation more spiritual and meaningful.

Complex patterns

Mandalas and yantras are traditional meditation tools used in Buddhist and Hindu traditions. These complex geometric patterns may be painted or made from colored glass, flowers, or sand and can be studied and contemplated as a means to reaching a meditative state. Throughout the book you will find full-page color depictions of examples from a range of traditions.

Finally, the book includes step-by-step photographs of exercises from contemplative practices including yoga, tai chi, and chi kung. These exercises are considered by many to be the equivalent of meditation, offering the same benefits of relaxation and focused awareness. All the exercises shown are simple and easy to follow, but please consult your doctor before beginning any exercise program (see the note on page 4), especially if you are pregnant or have a health condition.

The symbols in this book

 Work with this exercise now This symbol guides you to the correct page, tells you how to proceed with the exercise, and includes the appropriate CD track number, if applicable, and the page number on which you will find the script.

 I'm not there yet This offers reasons why you may be feeling this way and suggests ways you can work with other exercises to help open you to this new form of meditation.

 Illustration This symbol indicates the page on which you will find a practical or helpful image to accompany an exercise. It may show a meditation posture or method of breathing or offer you a visual aid, such as a mandala, to fix your gaze on.

 When to do this exercise This suggests a time of day or a situation in life when this meditation might be beneficial.

 Work with the CD now This symbol tells you when you need to turn on the CD and which track to select. If you would like to follow the script to the CD, turn to the pages indicated in the Inspirations chapter on pages 242–249.

Glossary of terms

Adept
A dedicated spiritual practitioner; a highly skilled meditator.

Boddhisattva
An enlightened being in Buddhism, who refrains from entering Nirvana out of compassion in order to help others achieve enlightenment.

Chi kung/Qigong Kung and gong
are Chinese terms meaning "work" or "practice" and *chi* or *qi* refer to "energy." This form of "energy cultivation" is an ancient Chinese system of postures, exercises, breathing techniques, and meditation designed to improve and enhance the body's energy.

Concentration
In meditation, focus and concentration on a single object or on the breath is used as a way of calming the mind.

Equanimity
One of the "Four Immeasurables" of Buddhism; the other three are loving-kindness, sympathetic joy, and compassion. As a meditative practice, equanimity helps develop the ability to love unconditionally.

Mandala
Originally a visual aid for meditation used in Tantric Hinduism and Buddhism, a mandala is a two-dimensional diagram representing the three-dimensional universe and sacred abode of a deity.

Mantra
A syllable, word, or group of words in the sacred Sanskrit language that when uttered out loud, silently, or written are thought to bring about spiritual transformation.

Mindfulness
Becoming aware, in an objective way, of the body, emotions, thoughts and attitudes, and the world around you. Mindfulness plays a central role in the teaching of Buddhism.

Yantra
A two- or three-dimensional visual aid for meditation in the Hindu tradition; it depicts the meditator's journey to enlightenment.

Work with the CD now Play Track 1 of the CD as you lie down and get comfortable. To prepare for the peace, tranquility, and insight that meditation can bring to your life, listen to the relaxing music. Close your eyes and let your worries and cares go for the moment, allowing the sounds to wash over you. When the music ends, open your eyes and notice how even this small meditative exercise can have a profound effect on your body and your mood.

WHAT IS
MEDITATION?

The story of meditation

Meditation is a mental discipline that helps you let go of your normal, reflexive thinking mind so that a deeper state of awareness, insight, and relaxation can emerge. Meditation has its roots in antiquity and continues to be an aspect of many religions. It is also practiced in secular contexts for self-development and healing. As you will discover in this book, meditation encompasses a wide range of practices that emphasize different goals. Among them are spiritual development and reaching a higher state of consciousness, better focus and concentration, creativity, self-awareness and insight, physical and emotional healing, and stress reduction and relaxation.

The first meditation manual

As you start your journey into meditation it may help you to know there are many who have gone before you. The first written record of meditation is the 5,000 year-old Indian *Vigyana Bhairava Tantra*. It contains 112 meditation techniques for realizing one's true self, written as a series of beautiful poems. All 112 meditations are answers given by the Hindu god Shiva to questions from the goddess Devi regarding the nature of reality. Instead of answering her questions directly, Shiva gives Devi meditation techniques so that she might experience the answers for herself.

Building on the Hindu tradition *Shakyamuni Buddha*, who lived in India 2,500 years ago, gave up his privileged life to pursue spiritual knowledge through meditation, and became the Buddha, or the "Awakened One." It is through meditation that he gained enlightenment. He taught concentration and mindfulness meditation to help others achieve wisdom, and encouraged people to generate love and compassion for all living beings. He taught that meditation can lead—one person at a time—to bliss and to the end of human suffering as we know it.

Meditation in the East

Across Asia, meditation practices arose suited to the belief system and topography of various regions. In India, the Hindu tradition advocated the practice of yoga which combined ethical conduct, physical poses, breathing techniques, spiritual study, and meditation for the goal of spiritual development. In Tibet, visualization practices equipped adepts to sit in meditation for long periods in cool temperatures. In China a number of meditative practices developed to enhance longevity, as described in the *I Ching* and the *Tao Te Ching*. The internal martial arts such as tai chi and chi kung are considered "moving meditations," and have their roots in Taoist practice. Across the Islamic world, five times a day believers perform the salat, a meditation focusing the mind and heart on God.

Kneeling Pose

Egyptian Pose

Meditation in the West

Contemplative techniques have been part of Christianity since the desert fathers in Egypt practiced a form of recitation of a prayer or holy words on the breath as a means of drawing closer to God. They also advocated the practice of *Lectio Divina* or "divine reading." This was a practice of prayer and scriptual reading which was typically performed for one continuous hour daily, in which Christians would read the Bible slowly and carefully in order to ponder the deeper meaning of each verse and promote communion with God. The popular contemporary form of meditation known as Centering Prayer, also places emphasis on interior quiet in order to experience God's presence.

Worshippers in the Catholic, Orthodox Christian, and Jewish traditions continue to follow age-old distinct meditation techniques as do followers of Native American spirituality, while Pagans and Wiccans forge new ways of meditating, often adapting or building upon ideas from Eastern traditions.

Secular meditation

Throughout history meditation has been used as a method for spiritual development, but religious affiliation is not a prerequisite for practicing any form of meditation, even if it originated in a religious context. Many secular meditations have risen in popularity in the modern era, such as Transcendental Meditation (TM) and Mindfulness Based Stress Reduction (MBSR), which are validated by scientific study rather than religion.

During the 1960s and 1970s, interest in meditation grew in the West thanks to celebrities such as the Beatles who travelled to India in search of spiritual enlightenment. In turn, teachers of Eastern meditation migrated to the West. In 1975, Dr. Herbert Benson of Harvard Medical School began to explore the potential medical benefits that meditation has to offer. Others have continued the scientific study of meditation, which is now regularly practiced in hospital settings and clinics to promote healing and stress reduction.

Four types of meditation

Although there are numerous meditation traditions—Eastern and Western, religious and secular—most meditation techniques fall into four ways of working with the mind. In this book we will explore all four kinds of meditation.

Using a focus

The first technique involves learning to focus and concentrate. By training the mind to focus on an object—such as a candle or an image, on the breath, or on a movement such as walking— you become aware of your normal uncontrolled thinking patterns and eventually learn to relax and quiet your mind. The ability to calm and stabilize the mind is a good beginning practice and important as a basis for mindfulness meditation.

Using mindfulness

The second technique involves learning about yourself and the world around you. This is called mindfulness, insight, or awareness meditation. In this type of meditation, you become aware of the content of your mind and the subtle feelings in your body. Then you begin to observe the mental habits and patterns that may be holding you back in life. Through mindfulness you learn to be mentally present—aware of what you are doing and thinking, and aware also of the world around you—while maintaining a nonjudgmental and compassionate attitude.

Using a topic

The third way to meditate is to contemplate a topic. The early Christians for example meditated on passages of *The New Testament*, while Tibetan Buddhists meditate on topics such as compassion, loving-kindness, patience, or generosity. Often spiritual adepts of all traditions East and West meditate on death, not to be morbid, but to help recognize the fleeting quality and precious nature of human life. This helps practitioners to sort out priorities and make good use of their time.

Using the senses

The fourth type of meditation engages the senses. Using sight to harness the mind's ability to imagine or visualize you

can create the kind of mind and reality you want to inhabit. Using your sense of hearing and your voice you can practice chanting and mantra recitation and listen to music and the sounds of nature to bring about meditative states that hasten healing and spiritual development.

Easy Pose

The benefits of meditation

Meditation is profoundly beneficial for body, mind, and spirit. For example, simply meditating on your breath can lower your blood pressure, slow your heart rate, and reduce anxiety. As an adjunct to allopathic or complementary medical treatment, meditation has been shown to promote healing from various illnesses, including cancer and heart disease. It can manage pain and prevent illness by helping you stay physically balanced and healthy. Meditation helps create mental contentment, peace, and joy, too, which in turn helps promote health and longevity.

Researcher Richard Davidson discovered that concentrative meditation—focusing the mind on one object like the breath—synchronizes brainwaves, positively affecting body and mind. Practicing this technique stills the mind and helps you develop mental skills useful in all areas of life. Having the ability to focus and concentrate when you need to, for example, promotes success in your career and makes life easier at work for yourself and co-workers. Being able to give your full attention to friends and family improves your relationships by helping them feel listened to, respected, and loved.

Compassion and spirituality

After you learn to still your mind, practicing mindfulness meditation helps you to identify negative habitual thoughts and mental patterns that may be keeping you feeling stuck and unfulfilled. This form of meditation helps you to identify and relax chronic body tension that may prevent you from experiencing the joy and happiness you desire. Through mindfulness meditation you can learn to be less emotionally reactive, cut down on judgment and self-hatred, and increase compassion for yourself and others.

Meditation can enhance your spiritual life, too. Spirituality refers to the life-force and intelligent energy that pervades the universe. You may call this force God, Buddha, Christ, or your higher power. Whether you choose to have a formal religious life or not, meditation can help you explore the deeper meaning of your existence: exploring your connection to all living beings and discovering your destiny and the sacred nature of reality.

Perfect Pose

The meditating brain

The brain functions by using four kinds of brainwaves. Beta waves dominate when we are thinking, working, or conversing; alpha or theta brainwaves are present during relaxation, daydreaming, and creative activities. Delta brainwaves occur during deep, dreamless sleep. During meditation, our brainwaves change from beta to the slower, more relaxing alpha or theta.

Meditation has been shown to cause physical changes in specific areas of the brain. In 2002, Dr. Andrew Newberg, a researcher at the University of Pennsylvania, linked meditation to increased activity in the left prefrontal cortex, an area of the brain associated with concentration, planning, and positive feelings. Another researcher, Paul Ekman at the University of California San Francisco Medical Center, found that mindfulness meditation "tames" the amygdala, the primitive area of the brain responsible for the fight-or-flight reflex—the one that takes over when you feel in danger or threatened. His research found that experienced Tibetan Buddhist meditators were less likely than most people to be emotionally reactive, or get flustered and angry.

Meditation also seems to affect the size and health of certain areas of the brain. Researchers in a joint study at Harvard and Yale Universities and the Massachusetts Institute of Technology discovered that meditation not only causes increased activity, but also increased thickness in the left and right prefrontal cortex. This increase, they found, was more pronounced in older meditators, suggesting that meditation might offset age-related thinning of the cortex.

Meditation and depression

In a study reported in March 2009, Dr. Bradley Peterson of Columbia University found that cortical thinning is associated with depression. His team discovered that people with a family history of depression appear to have brains that are 28 percent thinner in the right cortex than those with no known family history of the disease. Those with additional cortical thinning

Meditation pose using a cushion

in the left hemisphere of the brain went on to develop the symptoms of clinical depression or anxiety.

Depressed people often find it hard to concentrate or remember facts and feel as if their brain is "foggy"; they may not pick up on social cues that do not match their own depressed world-view. These symptoms were once considered a response to depression, however this study shows that they may actually be a result of cortical thinning, and so a cause of depression. Dr. Peterson recommends the use of coaching, psychotherapy, and medication to prevent further deterioration of cortical brain tissue. But, according to the researchers in the Harvard, Yale, and the Massachusetts Institute of Technology study, meditation may not only prevent further deterioration but could reverse cortical thinning, thus helping to avoid or heal depression.

Besides generating pleasant beta brainwaves, taming the flight-or-fight area of the brain, and stimulating activity and growth of the frontal cortex,

meditation can foster positive emotions. Meditators who meditate on feelings of love and compassion can actually change their brain circuits. In a study conducted at the University of Wisconsin Madison published in 2008, researchers using functional magnetic resonance imaging (fMRI) revealed that subjects who had long-term experience of meditating on compassion dramatically enhanced the areas of the brain that detect feelings and emotion.

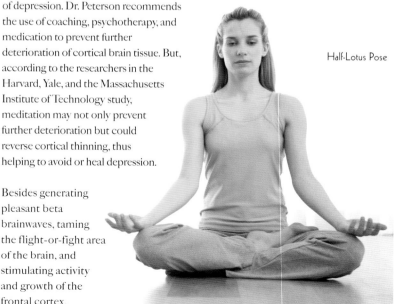

Half-Lotus Pose

The meditating body

Two important skills will greatly enhance your experience of meditation: the ability to relax your body and the ability to breathe deeply, making full use of your diaphragm. When you meditate it is important to sit (or recline) in a way that enhances relaxation, deep breathing, and energy-flow throughout your body. There are tried and true meditation postures that you can learn to enhance your meditation experience detailed on pages 29–32 along with a few items that you can buy to support you physically in your practice. Finally, setting aside a special place for meditation will be of great help in your journey.

Relaxation

Learning to relax your body sounds straightforward, but may be harder than you think. Most of us carry chronic tension in our bodies, especially around the shoulder and neck areas. When you begin to learn progressive relaxation in the Body Scan exercise on page 34, you will discover where you hold tension in your body and learn to release it. This relaxation exercise will enhance or even transform your meditation practice.

 Work with this exercise now Turn to Exercise 1: Body Scan on page 34 and follow the instructions. Keep your CD player within reach set to play Track 2. Lie down on your bed to practice, or lie on a mat on the floor in a quiet, warm place where you won't be disturbed.

Breathing

Like many people, you may be a shallow breather. In other words, you take small breaths that do not fully fill your lungs. This condition is not only bad for your health, but affects your ability to relax and center yourself. The lungs sit on top of the diaphragm. When you inhale, the diaphragm contracts and flattens as it moves downward against your internal organs, allowing the lungs to expand to receive fresh air. When you exhale, the diaphragm relaxes, moving upward against the lungs and helping to expel stale air. You will learn to breathe more fully by using your diaphragm properly in the following exercise.

Physical supports

Since most traditions recommended that you sit to meditate, a variety of cushions and other supports have developed over the centuries to aid the practice. Consider buying one to support *your* meditation. Cushions come in all shapes, sizes, and colors, and are stuffed with a variety of materials. Look at what is available online or in stores that sell meditation or yoga supplies. If possible, try them out before buying to see which works best for you. If you buy a meditation cushion, you may like to invest in a larger, flat mat, often called a *zabuton* that goes beneath your cushion. This raises your cushion a little higher off the ground and also protects your ankles. If you are unable to sit on the floor on a cushion, make sure you have a simple straight-backed chair to sit on.

Meditation postures

The traditional Eastern meditation posture involves sitting cross-legged on a cushion on the floor. There are many variations of this posture from yoga's *Padmasana*, the full Lotus Pose for the very flexible among us to the more attainable Half-lotus Pose, or simply sitting with your legs crossed comfortably at the ankles (see page 23). It is perfectly fine to sit on a straight-backed chair if you find sitting on a cushion too difficult. Some meditations are best practiced lying down. In all postures the back is kept straight yet relaxed. In the following exercise, experiment with what posture or postures work best for you.

 Work with this exercise now Turn to Exercise 2: Belly Breathing on page 38 and follow the instructions. Visualize your diaphragm moving as you breathe.

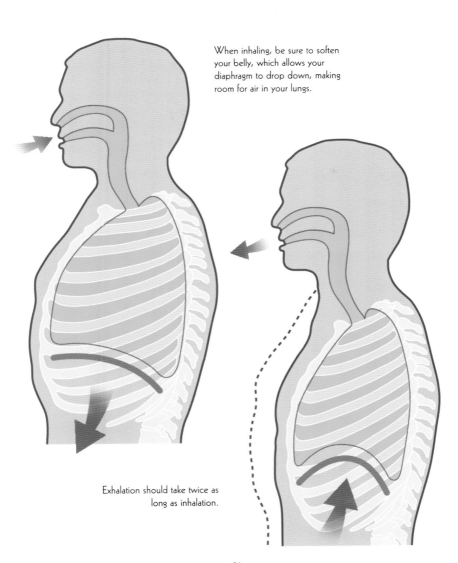

When inhaling, be sure to soften
your belly, which allows your
diaphragm to drop down, making
room for air in your lungs.

Exhalation should take twice as
long as inhalation.

Creating a special place for meditation

Try to find a special, quiet place in which to meditate. If you have an extra room, you can turn that into your meditation space. If not, set aside a space in a corner of your bedroom or living room, or create a temporary space just for the times when you meditate. Whether your sacred space is temporary or permanent, by creating a special place that is pleasing and serene, you honor your intention to meditate and make it easier to maintain a daily practice.

 Work with this exercise now Turn to Exercise 3: Basic Sitting Posture on page 42. Follow the instructions to try out the poses for yourself. On Track 3 of the CD you will find additional instructions for the traditional Buddhist seven-point cross-legged posture, which will suit people who can already sit comfortably in Half- or Full Lotus Pose.

PREPARATORY EXERCISES

The exercises on the following pages will give you a sound base for embarking on your meditation practice. The guidance on relaxing, sitting, breathing, and approaching your meditation can be applied to any exercise in this book.

Relaxing my body

Relaxation reduces stress and prepares you for meditation. The body's bio-chemistry responds in the same way to real or imagined threat, releasing chemicals into the bloodstream that tell body and brain to get ready for danger. However if you do not run away or physically fight the stressor, the stress chemicals aren't released and continue to surge through your bloodstream, causing harm to body and brain. This exercise negates those responses, teaching you how it feels to be physically relaxed and mentally at peace.

Exercise 1 BODY SCAN
CD REFERENCE TRACK 2 (TO FOLLOW THE SCRIPT, TURN TO PAGE 242)

  When to do this exercise Try practicing whenever you need to relax, to prepare you for meditation or to help you sleep.

- **Put on loose, comfortable clothing** and remove any jewelry and your watch. Then lie on your bed or on the floor in a place where you will not be disturbed. If the room is cool, cover yourself with a light blanket to preserve body heat.

- **Read the text on pages 242–243** and when ready turn on Track 2 and follow the guided meditation.

My body scan experience

Questions to consider
How did I feel before the exercise and how do I feel now?
What areas of my body seemed to hold most tension?
Was I aware that I held tension in those parts of my body before this exercise?
Did I experience any emotion when I relaxed areas of my body that were
previously tense?

Date _____ Time _____

_____

_____

_____

_____

_____

Date _____ Time _____

_____

_____

_____

_____

_____

Date _____ Time _____

_____

_____

_____

_____

_____

_____

_____

Date _____ Time _____

_____

_____

_____

_____

_____

_____

_____

Date _____ **Time** _____

_____

_____

_____

_____

_____

_____

_____

_____

_____

Date _____ **Time** _____

_____

_____

_____

_____

_____

_____

_____

_____

_____

Breathing more deeply

In many of the meditations in this book I recommend that you breathe "into the belly." Belly breathing focuses you on using the diaphragm to expand and contract the belly, which helps to deepen the breath. Many of us simply expand the rib-cage, which results in a shallow breath. This exercise also helps to counter stress and the ideal of a flat, hard stomach.

 ## Exercise 2 BELLY BREATHING
CD REFERENCE TRACK 1 OR TRACK 6 (OPTIONAL)

 Illustration See page 31 for illustrations showing the position of the lungs and diaphragm. Note where the diaphragm is located and how it functions when you breathe deeply.

 When to do this exercise Before any meditation or whenever you would like to practice breathing in a more healthful, calming, and energizing way. It is useful at times of stress, which cause us to take shallow breaths into the upper chest, or anger, when we tend to inhale and hold the breath.

- **Lie down and get comfortable.** Suck in your belly and try to inhale deeply. With your belly contracted you should feel a great deal of tension and difficulty in breathing, forcing you to take frequent, shallow breaths. When the belly is tight, the diaphragm has a difficult time moving downward because it is resisted by contracted abdominal muscles and internal organs.

- **Place one hand on your belly** and one on your chest. Now soften your belly and let it expand as you take a long slow breath in. Feel your diaphragm drop, as first the lower then the upper part of your lungs fills with air. When you soften your belly, allowing it to expand as you inhale, your organs drop, allowing the diaphragm to more easily contract downward.

- **Exhale slowly, allowing your belly** to settle into its normal position. As your diaphragm relaxes and moves upward feel your belly settle back into its normal place.

- **Practice belly breathing** in this way for ten minutes. Bear in mind that exhaling for twice as long as you inhale helps the body relax and let go of the "fight-or-flight" stress responses. Sit up carefully after ending your practice.

My belly-breathing experience

Questions to consider
How did breathing into my belly affect me physically?
How did breathing into my belly affect me mentally?

Date _____ Time _____

_____

_____

_____

_____

_____

_____

Date _____ Time _____

_____

_____

_____

_____

_____

_____

Date _____ Time _____

_____

_____

_____

_____

_____

_____

_____

_____

Date _____ Time _____

_____

_____

_____

_____

_____

_____

_____

_____

Sitting to meditate

You can sit on the floor to meditate, choosing one of the postures illustrated on pages 19–28, but it is also fine to sit on a straight-backed chair. If you choose to sit cross-legged, use a small meditation cushion or a folded bed pillow to raise your bottom 4–6 inches from the ground. If you are using a chair, sit on the front half of the seat and place both feet flat on the ground about 1 foot apart. Sit up straight without using the back of the chair for support while, at the same time, keeping your shoulders relaxed.

 ## Exercise 3 BASIC SITTING POSTURE

CD REFERENCE TRACK 3 (TO FOLLOW THE SCRIPT, TURN TO PAGE 244). THIS IS OPTIONAL BECAUSE IT GIVES ADDITIONAL INSTRUCTIONS FOR THE MORE CHALLENGING TRADITIONAL BUDDHIST SEVEN-POINT SITTING POSTURE.

 Illustration See pages 19–28 for illustrations showing how to position your legs in Kneeling, Egyptian Pose, Easy Pose, Perfect Pose, or the Half Lotus Pose then sit in one of these positions before starting the exercise.

 When to do this exercise The following basic posture can be used in most of the meditations in this book.

- **Sit on the floor** in one of the poses shown in the illustrations on pages 19–28 or on a chair. Gently sway your body from side to side until your spine feels centered. Lengthen your spine into its natural curve by imagining you have a string attached to the crown of your head and that it is being pulled gently from above. Relax your stomach muscles so that your abdomen becomes soft and rounded and the small of your back gently curves forward. Scan your body and release any tension or tightness.

- **Check that your head is level**, your shoulders are relaxed, and your ears are parallel with your shoulders. Align your nose directly over your navel, and slightly tuck in your chin.

- **Focus your eyes** in the space about 3–4 feet in front of you, lowering your eyelids slightly at a 45-degree angle.

- **Place your left hand** on top of your right hand with both palms facing upward and your thumbs raised slightly and just touching. The sides of your little fingers should rest against your lower abdomen about 3 inches below your navel.

- **Close your mouth** and rest your tongue against the roof of your mouth. Let the tip of your tongue rest gently against your upper front teeth. Remain in this position until the end of the meditation. Then unfold your hands and legs and stretch carefully before slowly standing up, raising your head last.

My basic sitting posture experience

Questions to consider
Did I have difficulty with the basic posture?
Did I try the classic seven-point posture from the CD?
Was I able to complete this more advanced posture?

Date _____   Time _____

_____

_____

_____

_____

_____

_____

Date _____   Time _____

_____

_____

_____

_____

_____

_____

Date _____ Time _____

_____

_____

_____

_____

_____

_____

_____

Date _____ Time _____

_____

_____

_____

_____

_____

_____

_____

Thinking about motivation

The Dalai Lama often says "motivation is everything." In other words, *why* you do something is as important as *what* you do. Two people can perform the same action and have a different experience, according to their motivation or intention. For example, one person may give to charity with the genuine motivation of helping those in need; another may give to bolster a reputation or evade taxes. The first person experiences the joy of giving and enhances his or her ability to be generous. The second loses out on the good feelings that come with generosity and suffers the anxiety of depending on social status and material wealth for a sense of self-worth. Before meditation, setting a positive intention enhances its benefits.

Exercise 4 INTENTION AND DEDICATION

When to do this exercise Try to set your intention and dedicate your effort before every meditation. You can also set your intention and dedicate your effort for any other activity in life.

- **Set your intention for working** on the exercises in the book by stating to yourself why you are doing the exercise. The introduction to each exercise will give you a clue to the appropriate intention. You could also set an intention that extends beyond your meditation session into your everyday life; you might vow, for example, to be a less angry person.

- **After setting your intention**, sit quietly for a few minutes. Then follow the meditation.

- **On ending your meditation**, dedicate your efforts to a higher purpose. This helps to "lock in" positive results. You could dedicate your meditation to relieve the suffering of children around the world, for example, or to support a friend in difficulty, or simply to help yourself. This "bookend" approach to setting intention and dedicating your efforts helps you to stay conscious of why you are meditating and can turbo-charge your practice.

My intention and dedication experience

Questions to consider
How did the practice of setting my intention and dedicating my effort change
my feelings about working with the meditations in this book?
As I move forward with my meditation journey, which intentions and
dedications seem most beneficial and/or inspiring?

Date _____ Time _____

_____

_____

_____

_____

_____

_____

Date _____ Time _____

_____

_____

_____

_____

_____

_____

MEDITATIONS FOR
CALMING THE MIND

Is your mind out of control?

If you are like most human beings on the planet, at some point in life you will have experienced a crisis. Perhaps a relative or dear friend died. Or you lost something important—a relationship with a lover or friend or a job you needed to pay your bills, or you lost your home to a fire. What you knew to be secure and all your future plans evaporated; it felt as if the ground had disappeared from beneath you. One day everything seemed normal, then your thoughts and your life were thrown into chaos.

Racing thoughts and mental ruts

In that darkest of times, you may have experienced a sense of your mind being out of control. Thoughts raced through your head and you had no way to stop them. It was as if your mind had a mind of its own. You may have had trouble sleeping as your thoughts kept you awake, leading to physical and mental exhaustion. After a few days or weeks the shock may have worn off as you picked up the pieces and tried to move on. Your mind eventually stopped racing and returned to its normal state, jumping from one thought to the next.

We are so used to the mind jumping from one thought to another that this seems familiar and natural. We may also revisit thoughts over and over again. For example, if we are chronically worried about money or weight, our thoughts tend to dwell on those topics. It may seem as if we have worn little ruts into the brain from going over the same material every day. In a way this feels comforting, because it is familiar. We know who we are because we know our thoughts. Or so we think until we start to meditate and find out who we really are.

The dance of projection and avoidance

All of us develop mental habits, for example we may have a tendency to see the world as dangerous and view any stranger as untrustworthy. Or we put on rose-colored glasses and appear warm and receptive, yet we find ourselves taken advantage of at every turn. Everyone else may be able to see the truth, but we miss all the cues. Or perhaps we see faults in everyone that are remarkably similar to our own,

unacknowledged, faults. Meditation can help us to see and acknowledge who we really are.

If we are afraid of something—a person or a social situation—we may go into avoidance mode. We find ways to avoid thinking about what frightens us and instead engage in mental gymnastics to put off facing the inevitable. Engaging the mind in surfing the internet or watching television, we engage in magical thinking. If we just avoid thinking about what frightens us, we won't have to face that fear. Again, meditation helps us to face the fear and find out that it is more approachable than we thought.

We have to think to be able to function in daily life, but we can pay too much attention to our thoughts. For example, if we are attracted to people, we may put them on a pedestal, being absolutely sure they are perfect in every way. Or if we think we are unworthy, we become so. We attach ourselves so much to our thoughts that they become part of our identity. We implicitly trust our observations, even though many studies show that if five people witness a crime each may have a dramatically different view of what happened. Meditation gives us some welcome perspective.

A calm mind is your first step to peace and enlightenment

The Eastern sages of long ago discovered that we are much more than our thoughts. Hindus, Taoists, and Buddhists all advocated practicing meditation to calm the mind and still obsessive and uncontrolled thinking. They understood that we are beings capable of profound peace and serenity, of vast depth and richness, and even of bliss and enlightenment. But to reach the depths of that ocean of knowledge and experience we need first to calm the waves on the surface—the thoughts and emotions that keep the waters churned. When the water is still and clear we can then see into the depths. By practicing the concentrative meditation techniques outlined in this chapter you can learn to calm your mind, even at moments of great stress, and begin to harness its power and energy to improve your life.

To calm the mind, focus on the breath

Concentration meditation is the first of the four kinds of meditation you will meet in this book. Also called concentrative meditation, this is an ancient technique to calm the mind. By training yourself to concentrate on an object such as a candle, or on an image or on your breath, you become aware of your normal uncontrolled thinking patterns and eventually learn to relax and quieten your mind. You can also increase your ability to maintain focused attention, an important skill that makes everything more enjoyable and productive, from driving and working to playing an instrument or conversing with a friend. Concentrative meditation benefits health by calming the nerves, improving emotional balance, and aiding sleep. When life presents difficulties, as it will, you will be better able to weather the storm if you practice this technique.

In the Hindu, Buddhist, and Taoist spiritual traditions, being able to achieve mental quiescence is a prerequisite for spiritual growth—this means maintaining a state of mind that is quiet and still, yet alert and aware. The Buddha described breath meditation as a way not only to quiet the mind but also to purify it of any negativity or disturbing thoughts. He compared it to an unexpected cloudburst in the hot season that disperses and washes away the dry dust and dirt swirling around. Other Buddhist sages have described the breath as a horse and the person meditating as its rider. By learning to ride the breath you tame the wild horse of your mind. Others still compare a quiet, calm mind to a tool, such as a microscope in a lab or a telescope in an observatory, used to investigate yourself and the universe.

Resting on your breath

In the exercises for calming the mind on pages 66–75, you use the breath as a focus for meditation. Your breath is always with you; it is a part of you, and at any time you can use it to meditate. Breathing represents being alive in the immediate moment, and by resting your

mind on your breath you learn how to stay present and awake to what is happening in and around you. Paying attention to the steady flow of your breath will soothe your mind, reduce its habit of jumping from one thought to another, and allow you to relax. The Basic Breath Meditation on page 66 teaches you simply to concentrate and focus on the breath. This is not a concentration that is full of effort or a feeling of bearing down on the breath. Rather it is light and gentle. When you try to focus on your breath, thoughts will inevitably intervene: a sound outside will distract you and emotions will arise. The natural curiosity and playfulness of your mind will generate all kinds of thoughts. Before you know it you may be lost in thinking about a friend, then what your friend would think of you meditating. Or your mind may jump to your upcoming dentist appointment or the bag of snacks waiting for you in the kitchen.

When those interruptions happen— and they will—simply bring your focus back to your breath. You may do this hundreds of times within one meditation session. There is no need to reprimand yourself when your mind wanders. Just bring your mind back to your breath as you would bring a wandering child back to your side, with gentleness, love, and affection. With time and practice your mind will calm down and a sense of peace and serenity will emerge.

 Work with this exercise now Find a quiet place where you will be undisturbed and can meditate for at least 20 minutes. Then turn to Exercise 5: Basic Breath Meditation on page 66 and follow the instructions.

I'm not there yet If this seems complicated and you are worried about "doing it right," try not to be. Meditation is a journey not a destination. To relax before your meditation, practice the Body Scan exercise on page 34.

The three activities of breath meditation

There are three activities that support breath meditation: becoming familiar with your breathing; remembering to stay focused on the breath; and avoiding distraction. Your mind has a natural, stable nature, but this is hiding behind the noise of continuous thought. The true nature of your mind is inherently spacious, calm, and quiet. To begin to access that stable, calm mind you need only focus on your breath.

Become familiar with your breath

In the beginning, you may be unfamiliar with your breathing because you have always taken it for granted. Until now it has been something in the background, an automatic process that takes care of itself. Like many of us, you may take shallow breaths. If you are hunched over a computer all day, you may actually breathe very little, which contributes to stress and fatigue. Also, you may not even know how your breathing actually works. The Belly Breathing exercise on page 38 introduced you to the diaphragm and the importance of being able to fully fill and release air from your lungs. So number one priority is becoming familiar with the breath itself, befriending it and learning about its qualities and rhythms.

Countering boredom

At first, even though it seems like a good idea, it may seem boring to focus just on your breath. After all, you may wonder, what is so great about that? By practicing for at least 20 minutes at a time and becoming familiar with your breath and its rhythm, you will begin to relax and find enjoyment in the mental stability it brings. When you begin to experience the joys of a quiet mind, you will want to continue to explore what a breath-focus has to offer.

Besides calming your mind, your breath has a tremendous power to facilitate healing. If you are sick, meditating on your breath while using your diaphragm to ensure a full inhalation and exhalation will bring oxygen and healing energy to every part of your body. Your breath is a

key to your physical and spiritual life-force, and becoming familiar with it not only brings mental quiescence but also enhances physical energy and vitality. It is through your breath that you take in the life-giving energy of the universe.

Stay focused on your breath

Remembering to stay focused on your breath is about being present in the moment and knowing what you are doing—in this case, meditating on your breath. If you get caught up in your thoughts, you forget to meditate. Remembering to come back to your breath over and over again builds familiarity with the breath itself and will bring you the calm mind you are

seeking. More importantly, remembering to come back to your breath helps you to stay in the present moment and remain fully aware of what you are doing. This quality of being fully present to yourself and the moment will not only transform your meditation but has the potential to transform your life.

Avoid distractions

The ongoing practice of avoiding distraction, as you hold your mind to your breath, will eventually allow you to keep a focus without much effort. When a thought arises, your mind will no longer run off like a wild horse. You will notice the thoughts and distractions, but the stability and strength of your natural mind will seem more attractive. This is what is known as taming the mind. A strong, stable, clear, and fully present mind is a powerful tool to help you build whatever you want from life.

Work with this exercise now If you have already tried the Basic Breath Meditation on page 66, turn to Exercise 6: Three Activities of Breath Meditation on page 70 and follow the instructions.

I'm not there yet If focusing on the three activities seems a little overwhelming, just work with one of the activities at a time in separate sessions. There is no rush; you can work with all three activities in your own time and at your own pace.

Discovering your mind's natural state

If I am not thinking, than what is in my mind? Meditation throws up all manner of profound questions, such as does anything exist behind my thoughts and what is my mind's natural state? Breath meditation can point the way toward many answers.

In the third exercise in this chapter, Open, Spacious Mind on page 74, you still maintain a focus on your breath, but shift and split your focus slightly to observe each thought as it arises, passes by and then fades away. You imagine yourself stretched out on the grass on a beautiful day observing clouds passing by, one after another, against the backdrop of a clear blue sky. If you look to one side you see the clouds approaching, then you see them overhead, and finally they move on.

Just observe

The clouds are like your thoughts and emotions. Instead of becoming caught up with them and running with them, letting them alter your blood pressure and heart rate, you simply observe them, noticing how changeable and impermanent they are. You may also find yourself letting your eyes fall into the vast still blueness behind the clouds, something you may not have noticed before because you were so focused on the shapes of the clouds themselves.

In the same way, as you maintain your focus on your breath you can watch your thoughts come and go like clouds in the sky. After your mind settles in meditation, you can catch glimpses of the natural ground of your mind that exists behind the mental chatter of your thoughts and the roller coaster of your emotions. This is your mind in its natural state, beautiful, clear, blue, and spacious. And it is always there. So when life gets difficult and your mind is swirling with fears and projections, by focusing on your breath you can recall that something within you which is always still, calm, and supportive.

Work with this exercise now If you have already tried the Basic Breath Meditation on page 66, turn to Exercise 6: Three Activities of Breath Meditation on page 70 and follow the instructions.

I'm not there yet If you feel you will not be able to keep a mental distance from your thoughts and look on them as an observer, try spending more time practicing the Basic Breath Meditation (see page 66) and The Three Activities of Breath Meditation (see page 70).

Maintaining a calm mind

The peace and calm you find on your meditation cushion will greatly influence everything you do. Yet the stress and pace of daily life can easily undermine your efforts. The final exercise in this chapter, on pages 78–79, will help you explore ways to make changes in your life to help you maintain the serenity you enjoy during meditation.

It is within your power to exert control over what you take into your mind—from the people you mix with to the way you engage with the television, radio, internet, and reading material. The more you find peace and serenity in your meditation, the less you may want to expose yourself to the violence in the nightly news. You may also want to limit the time you spend with people who incite negative emotions in you, such as anger or jealousy. If you are addicted to food, drugs, alcohol, or the internet, you may find that your addictions undermine the calm and serenity you experience during meditation. And meditation may help you to find the internal strength to address those problem areas of your life.

 Work with this exercise now To bring calmness into your daily life by creating a kind, compassionate and a cheerful attitude toward yourself, turn to Exercise 8: Everyday, Peaceful Mind on page 78 and follow the instructions.

CONCENTRATION EXERCISES

The exercises on the following pages will help to cultivate a calm mind, a prerequisite for a deeper examination of yourself and the world around you. Having a calm and stable mind is the main ingredient in a happy and productive life.

Meditating on my breath

Meditation on the breath is an ancient, tried and true practice for calming the mind and lays down a wonderful foundation for other meditation practices. It can be a source of healing and inner peace. Before you begin, review the instructions on meditation postures on page 42 and choose a seated posture you can comfortably maintain without fidgeting.

 ## Exercise 5 BASIC BREATH MEDITATION
CD REFERENCE TRACK 4 (TO FOLLOW THE SCRIPT, TURN TO PAGE 245)

 Illustration To refresh your knowledge of how the diaphragm works, look at the illustration on page 31. See pages 19–28 for illustrations showing sitting positions.

 When to do this exercise If possible, practice at least once a day. Ideally, repeat once in the morning and once in the evening. You can also practice breath meditation spontaneously, wherever you are.

- **Find or create a place to meditate** that is quiet and comfortable. Choose a sitting meditation posture that you find comfortable (see page 42) and cover yourself with a shawl or blanket for warmth, if necessary.

- **Spend a few minutes practicing** a full belly breath (see page 38 if you need to recap this technique). When ready turn on Track 4 and follow the guided meditation.

- **Remember to check in** once in a while as you follow the guided meditation to see whether you are still fully relaxed. Check to see if your shoulders are relaxed and not slowly creeping up around your ears, or whether there is tension in any other part of your body.

- **Try to remain as still as possible** during the exercise. If it helps, imagine you are a mountain: still, quiet, and unmovable.

- **Remain vigilant** as you meditate until the end. Meditation is not about "spacing out" or drifting into drowsiness. Maintain an attitude of physical relaxation and alertness to reinforce this quality in your mind until you close your practice.

My basic breath meditation experience

Questions to consider
Did I find it difficult to maintain focus on my breath?
Did I feel any different after meditating for 20 minutes?

Date _____ Time _____

_____

_____

_____

_____

_____

_____

Date _____ Time _____

_____

_____

_____

_____

_____

_____

_____

Date _____ Time _____

_____

_____

_____

_____

_____

_____

_____

Date _____ Time _____

_____

_____

_____

_____

_____

_____

_____

_____

Practicing my three essentials

As you sit and meditate on your breath in this exercise, bring to mind the three activities that support breath meditation: becoming familiar with the breath, remembering to stay focused on the breath, and avoiding distraction. These activities may sound simple and obvious, but if you give them attention each time you meditate on your breath, they will enhance and deepen your practice.

 Exercise 6 THREE ACTIVITIES OF BREATH MEDITATION CD REFERENCE TRACK 4 (TO FOLLOW THE SCRIPT, TURN TO PAGE 245)

 Illustration See pages 19–28 for illustrations showing sitting positions.

 When to do this exercise Try this exercise after you have worked with Basic Breath Meditation on page 66 for a few sessions.

- **Adopt a comfortable sitting position** (see page 42) and remember to set your intention for this meditation (see page 46). Listen again to the guided breath meditation on Track 4 if you find this helpful.

- **For 6–7 minutes** focus only on becoming familiar with your breath.

- **For a further 6–7 minutes** remember to stay focused on your breath.

- **For the final 6–7 minutes** do not let any distractions disturb your focus on the breath. When they do, simply return quietly to your breath observation. At the end of your session, dedicate your efforts to whatever or whomever you wish.

My three activities of breath meditation experience

Questions to consider

Did the three activities help me to better understand breath meditation?

Which activity was most helpful?

Date _____ **Time** _____

_____

_____

_____

_____

_____

_____

Date _____ **Time** _____

_____

_____

_____

_____

_____

_____

Date _____ Time _____

_____

_____

_____

_____

_____

_____

_____

_____

_____

Date _____ Time _____

_____

_____

_____

_____

_____

_____

_____

_____

_____

Date _____ Time _____

_____

_____

_____

_____

_____

_____

_____

Date _____ Time _____

_____

_____

_____

_____

_____

_____

_____

Observing my thoughts

In this exercise, while maintaining focus on your breath you split your focus slightly and observe your thoughts as they arise, pass by, and then fade away.

This is a little more difficult than simply observing your breath. Again, do not worry about doing it perfectly, just give it a try and see what happens.

Exercise 7 OPEN, SPACIOUS MIND
CD REFERENCE TRACK 1 OR 6 (OPTIONAL)

 Illustration See pages 19–28 for illustrations showing sitting positions.

 When to do this exercise Try this exercise after you have worked with the Basic Breath Meditation (see page 66) and Three Activities of Breath Meditation (see page 70).

- Choose a sitting meditation posture that you find comfortable (see page 42). Your body should feel at ease throughout. Leave your eyes open and let your gaze fall in the space about 3–4 feet in front of you.

- Notice whether your mind is calm, alert, drowsy, or agitated. Now begin to stabilize your mind by counting 21 breaths. Place your attention at the place where your breath enters your nostrils. At the beginning of the inhalation, mentally count "one." Feel the sensations at your nose as your breathe in and out. As thoughts appear, mentally release them and return your attention to your breath.

- After counting 21 breaths, maintain a focus on your breath but begin to observe whatever arises in your mind. Watch your thoughts, images, emotions, and fantasies as they appear. Observe whatever comes up without caring whether it is there or not. Do not try to control what arises or engage with it.

- **Remain relaxed in your role** as observer. Continue to notice thoughts and images as they arise, come to the forefront of your mind then fade away. You are watching a display, as if on a screen, but are not influencing in any way what is shown to you. Accept whatever is there, whether it is peaceful or disturbing, puzzling or familiar. The important thing is not to grasp after anything. Simply observe and let go.

- **Whenever you find yourself** becoming engaged with your thoughts, return to a single-minded focus on your breath, stabilize your mind, then begin to watch your thoughts play out again with detachment.

- **Notice how your awareness** of your thoughts stays calm and clear, no matter which thoughts enter your mind. It is like sitting quietly and calmly in the corner of a room observing a group of noisy, boisterous people.

- **Sit in this meditative state** for at least 20 minutes. Notice how your mind settles when you are not identifying with the thoughts in your mind, judging them or trying to control them. See how peaceful and stable you are. This is your mind in its natural state. Savor it before bringing your practice to an end.

My open, spacious mind experience

Questions to consider
What did I discover about the nature of my thoughts?
What did I discover about the nature of my mind?
Did I experience at least a moment when my mind was resting in its natural state?
How did this feel?

Date _____ Time _____

_____

_____

_____

_____

_____

_____

_____

Date _____ Time _____

_____

_____

_____

_____

_____

_____

_____

Date _____ Time _____

_____
_____
_____
_____
_____
_____
_____
_____

Date _____ Time _____

_____
_____
_____
_____
_____
_____
_____
_____
_____

Bringing meditation into my life

The benefits of meditation are meant to extend beyond time spent "on the cushion." The following points, if practiced on a daily basis, will help you to export the serenity you experience while meditating into your daily life.

Exercise 8 EVERYDAY, PEACEFUL MIND

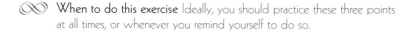 **When to do this exercise** Ideally, you should practice these three points at all times, or whenever you remind yourself to do so.

- **Try to avoid any material** on television, in the movies and print media or on the internet that arouse sensual craving or negative emotions such as greed, hatred, anxiety, or anger. If you are confronted with negativity in the media, try not to dwell on it, or to become emotionally "hooked" so that it upsets your natural equilibrium. There is nothing wrong with thinking about negative issues such as war or crime, but try not to let these things incite negative emotions in you. Engage in healthy sensuality and sexuality, but try to avoid becoming unbalanced or obsessed by it.

- **Although sometimes difficult** to do, stop yourself before reacting with anger or hatred when someone upsets you. Instead try to generate compassion for him or her. Think about how much you have in common with that person. For example, just like you, he or she suffers in many ways. Just like you, he or she desires happiness and wants to avoid pain. Just like you, that person sometimes gets on other people's nerves.

- **Bring the focus** you have on your breath in your meditation into your everyday life and work. When driving, try not to daydream. When engaged in conversation, learn to listen with your whole mind and heart. When cooking, cook, and when eating, eat without trying to do anything else. Try to bring a strong, stable, calm, fully present mind to everything you do.

My everyday, peaceful mind experience

Questions to consider
Did I make any changes to my daily routine in order to maintain a calm mind?
How did those changes affect me?

Date _____ Time _____

_____

_____

_____

_____

_____

_____

_____

Date _____ Time _____

_____

_____

_____

_____

_____

_____

_____

_____

MEDITATION FOR INCREASING MINDFULNESS

What is mindfulness?

In the previous chapter you learned about meditation practices for increasing focus and concentration and for calming the mind. You learned how to create a little mental space and peace in your normally busy and stressful life. In mindfulness meditation you work with the calm, stable mind you have cultivated through breath meditation to investigate your body, your feelings and attitudes, your mind and the content of your thoughts, and the world around you. With the tools of clear focus and stable concentration, you begin to observe yourself and see who you are, how you act, what you feel, and how you think. Through meditation you begin to know yourself in a different and deeper way than your normal way of perceiving yourself. Also, through mindfulness meditation you begin to look at the outside world and see how it relates to your inner world.

Mindfulness to relieve suffering
The purpose of applying mindfulness to these four aspects of experience (your body, feelings, mind, and environment) is to gain some insight into them—how

they function and how they exist. First, you will explore whether your body, feelings, mind, and the world around you, as you perceive it, is fixed and unchanging. Then you will look at whether any of these domains of your life can offer real and lasting happiness. Finally, you will look at the concepts "I" and "mine" and see how many of their attributions hold fast. The purpose of these explorations is to get to the root cause of everyday pain and suffering, which has a great deal to do with denying impermanence, looking for happiness in the wrong places, and seeing yourself as separate from others.

Mindfulness is a dedication to observing and seeing clearly, and being conscious and aware of what is happening in the present moment. The practice of mindfulness will help you to gain a deeper understanding of the connection between your thoughts and how they manifest in your actions. Over time, you will begin to discover which of your thoughts and actions bring happiness to yourself and those around you, and which lead to difficulties and suffering. You can then use

that insight to change unproductive ways of thinking, talking, and acting to productive ones. Dedicating yourself to this practice will diminish your conflict with others and make you a happier, more loving and compassionate person.

Mindfulness for a more productive, happier life

When you begin mindfulness meditation, you may discover how many daily activities you carry out automatically, without much awareness. Perhaps you go through your morning routine lost in thought about the day ahead. Then you get into the car, or walk to the bus, train, or subway barely noticing the people around you or the familiar landmarks en route. Mindfulness meditation can help you to remain more aware and present in everyday life. Rather than being distracted or lost in thought, you will find more to enjoy by learning to engage fully in every moment.

Mindfulness meditation leads you naturally to examine things you may think of as fixed, such as your personality and habits. You mistakenly may think of your personality and habits as the real *you*. You also may think of these aspects of yourself as unchangeable even though you have obviously evolved since childhood. Not realizing that you have the ability to change, you may continue each day trapped in habitual thoughts and behavior that does not serve you or the others in your life well. Through mindfulness meditation you can begin to recognize your patterns and perhaps choose a better alternative.

Before working with the meditation exercises for this chapter (see pages 98–111) be sure to practice the meditations for calming and stabilizing the mind from the previous chapter for a few weeks (see pages 66–79). Work especially on becoming fully comfortable with the Basic Breath Meditation (see page 66). Meditation practice is always a work in progress, so don't worry if you feel you are still struggling to calm your mind.

Being mindful of your body

In some spiritual traditions inner development means ignoring the body and moving toward a spiritual life identified exclusively with the mind. The body may be considered as defiled or a source of "sin," to be neglected and ignored. And yet we are all incarnated in a human body. Rather than being our enemy, I believe the body should be a source of pleasure, joy, inspiration, and spiritual development.

It is this body that equips us to work, love, and take care of ourselves. Through our bodies we communicate with others and appreciate the world around us, and we require our bodies to deepen our spiritual life through reading and learning, praying and meditating. So it is important to learn to pay attention to our bodies, to care for them well, and to keep them balanced physically and mentally. Becoming mindful of the beautiful instrument that is the body also helps us to reconnect with ourselves if we have been severed from our physical sensations through trauma or abuse.

Since the body and mind are not separate, awareness of the body provides a window onto our psychological state. The pain in the neck, the tense jaw, the tightness in the chest and lack of feeling in the groin area may point to areas of the psyche that need exploration and healing. Focusing closely on the body helps us to release areas of armoring we may not have been aware of, and helps us to move through the psychological blocks they may represent. By releasing physical and psychological blocks, we can deepen both our meditation practice and our spiritual development.

From physical to subtle body

Practising mindfulness meditation on the body involves moving from noticing physical sensations to becoming aware of more subtle energetic movements. You might start by noticing muscular tension and the sensation of pain or itching, for example, then become aware of your heartbeat, blood flow, and the sensation of energy moving through the body, and finally observe more minute sense perceptions. In order to learn to observe the world around you more clearly, you need also to experiment with seeing objects in your environment without the filters of possession (this is

mine), solidity (this is beautiful, permanent, unchanging), or desire (this person, thing, or situation will provide lasting happiness).

Everyday body awareness

After spending some time closely attending to your body in meditation, you will be able to extend your body awareness to everyday activities, such as walking, eating, speaking, driving, and observing the world through your senses. By paying close attention to your body you will learn more about your physical patterns and habits, and become able to change those that are harmful or negative. You may also become conscious of subtle changes that may indicate illness, and so be better able to maintain health and well-being.

 Work with this exercise now Turn to Exercise 9: Mindful Body Meditation on page 98. First read through the exercise noting the main points and then follow the instructions.

 I'm not there yet If you have anxiety about paying close attention to body sensations, try relaxing first by following the Body Scan exercise on page 34. Then try this exercise again. If any unpleasant emotions or memories arise, return your focus to your breath. If necessary, end the session and try again another time.

Being mindful of your emotions

Bringing mindfulness to your emotions and attitudes may be a little more challenging than focusing on your body. It helps to start by discriminating between emotions and attitudes. Your attitude in any situation can usually be boiled down to one of three: either you are attracted to or desire something or someone; you have an aversion to him, her, or it; or you are simply neutral or indifferent. Your emotional state is much more nuanced; you may respond to everyday situations with a complex mix of joy, desire, sadness, fear, jealousy, anger, and resentment. Your attitudes and emotions work together. For example, if you are attracted to someone, you may feel sad or jealous if that person shows interest in someone else. If you have aversion for someone, you may exaggerate that person's negative qualities and be quick to anger at anything they say or do. If you wait with strangers at the bus stop, you may not have any emotional reaction to them. You may not even notice them as you focus on your own thoughts.

How attitudes and feelings dovetail

Before practicing mindfulness of emotions, it helps to explore how emotions come into being. First, some kind of sensory stimulus or thought is required. This becomes the basis for a feeling. For example, your boss walks through your office door and you experience pleasure at her surprise visit, or have an immediate sense of fear because you know there are layoffs in the offing. If you feel pleasure, it may give rise to a desire for promotion. If you experience fear, that feeling may morph into aversion or even hatred as you sense that your boss is about to tell you that your employment is terminated.

Feelings and attitudes are often a stimulus to action. Pleasure at seeing your boss may lead you to invite her to sit down and have a cup of coffee. If you feel threat or aversion, you may let her stand there and feel uncomfortable as she delivers bad news. If anger arises, you may say something you regret. Usually the whole

sequence of events—a feeling that gives rise to an attitude (or vice versa) that gives rise to an action—is experienced seamlessly, and seems a part of us and our identity. Through meditation we can begin to take apart this mechanism and apply mindfulness to each stage.

Working with attitudes and emotions

First, through mindfulness meditation we can learn to pay close attention to our feelings and avoid any tendency to repress or suppress them. There is nothing wrong with emotions. The problems come when we identify strongly with a particular emotional state. For example, by thinking "I am angry" or "I am depressed" rather than removing the "I" and acknowledging that, yes, there is anger, sadness, or fear. By practicing mindfulness, we can begin to observe anger (or any other emotion) without judgment. We notice that emotions can arise, linger, and pass away, and that we don't have to get caught up in them or compulsively express them in a way that may be destructive to ourselves or others. We can also bring the same sense of detached exploration to our attitudes and realize that they represent a snapshot of where we are at the moment and that they will often change over time.

 Work with this exercise now Turn to Exercise 10: Being Mindful of My Attitudes and Emotions on page 102. First, read through the exercise noting the main points and instructions, then begin the meditation.

 I'm not there yet If you have concerns about triggering painful emotions, when practicing the meditation focus on a person or incident that is significant for you but not loaded with intense meaning.

Being mindful of your mind

We have now explored half of the four foundations of mindfulness: the mindfulness of body and the mindfulness of emotions. Now we will look at the third mindfulness: the mindfulness of mind. Here we work directly with the contents of the mind itself—thoughts, mental images, perceptions, emotions, feelings, memories, fantasies, and desires as they arise and fall away against the background of the mind's natural state. As we discovered on pages 50–53, in their normal state our minds are somewhat out of control. Through mindfulness of the contents of the mind itself, we can begin to pin the mind down to its basic presence in the moment.

Living the past, anticipating the future

In our usual mental state, we miss much of life. Instead, we tend to inhabit a state of having lived or will-be living. The mind is under the sway of the dictator of past memories or the seductress of future fantasies. We get lost in reliving events and conversations and rekindling powerful emotions we once felt. Or we lose ourselves in plans and dreams for the future, our brains firing in anticipation of that vacation on the beach or new car. There is nothing wrong with planning and anticipation, but often we invest too much energy and time in memories and dreams rather than enjoying life as it is now.

Examining the content of thoughts

Using the content of our thoughts as an object of meditation allows us to learn more about ourselves and the workings of the mind. We begin simply by observing our thoughts as they enter our awareness and then disappear. We try not to identify with them or get carried away by any one thought. Then, instead of simply watching them, we begin to observe patterns in the content. Is there an emotional tone that repeats, such as fear or anger? Do our thoughts seem to drift to money, health, food, or sex? Are we either planning the future or reliving memories? By examining thoughts we can begin to consciously choose their content, replacing negative or neurotic thinking patterns with more wholesome and productive ones.

We can also begin to touch on more existential questions, such as where thoughts come from, and whether they are "our" thoughts if we refrain from identifying with them. For example, do some thoughts seem to arise away from our control and, if so, from where? What is the nature of the ground from which all thoughts seem to arise and disappear into? Is that consciousness unchanging or impermanent? The practice of mindfulness of the mind brings us into a new relationship with our thoughts, one that helps us find happiness and the freedom to live fully right now.

 Work with this exercise now Turn to Exercise 11: Mindful Mind on page 106. First, read through the exercise, noting the main points, then follow the instructions.

Mindfulness of the true nature of everything

So far, we have explored mindfulness of the body, the emotions, and the mind. The last mindfulness is mindfulness of all phenomena, which is a fancy way of saying mindfulness of everything. In other words, it includes everything that arises within us and appears outside us. In this form of mindfulness meditation we try to discover some truths about how everything in life really is and how it functions.

In this exploration of mindfulness we revisit our usual tendency to grasp at everything in our reality. Grasping involves attraction and aversion. We want some things to stay with us (a feeling of romance with a new partner) and others to go away (the diagnosis of a serious health condition). In other words, we are always judging and interpreting what arises in the mind and in our experience, trying to hang on to what we like and push away what we find unpleasant or disturbing.

Everything is connected
This puts us on a collision course with reality because grasping after things, thoughts, and experiences assumes that they have an independent, solid, and unchanging existence. Yet in reality everything is dependent on everything else and not separate from it. So what seems to be negative may eventually turn out to be positive. For example, at a funeral, you reconnect with an old friend and end up marrying him or her. Or, conversely, you go on your dream vacation but lose your suitcase and all your belongings.

Our normal thinking also collides with reality because what we try to grasp is, by nature, in a constant state of flux. In other words, everything is in essence impermanent. Our relationships, our possessions, our experiences—all are impermanent. We grasp after things and people because we feel they will bring us happiness when, by nature, true happiness does not reside in us, other people, things, or situations. Mindfulness of the true nature of everything allows us to perceive this truth and understand that happiness is within us all.

Work with this exercise now Turn to Exercise 12: The True Nature of Everything on page 110. Read through the exercise and then follow the instructions

MINDFULNESS
EXERCISES

The following exercises will give you a taste of mindfulness meditation focused on your body, feelings, mind, and outside phenomena. Then mindfulness practice can become a part of your every waking moment.

My mindful body

This exercise shifts your focus to your body by asking you to observe its sense perceptions—physical sensations, sight, hearing, taste, touch. Before beginning this meditation, find a small natural object to observe during the exercise, such as a shell or a leaf. You will also need a cookie to eat during the session.

Exercise 9 MINDFUL BODY MEDITATION

 Illustration See pages 19–28 for illustrations showing sitting positions.

 **When to do this exercise** Practice mindfulness of the body when you are feeling disconnected with your body, having trouble taking care of yourself physically, or simply wish to experience your body in a new and beneficial way.

- **Choose a sitting meditation posture** that you find comfortable (see page 42). Keeping your eyes either closed or slightly open, relax any tense areas of your body and calm your mind by focusing on your breath for a few minutes.

- **Shift your focus from the breath** moving across your upper lip to a sensation in another part of your body, such as your knee or neck, or feel your bottom resting on the cushion or chair. Try to completely focus on that sensation without labeling it as pleasant or unpleasant. Do you feel tightness, burning, or an ache? Does it remain constant or is it changing? When thoughts intrude, bring your awareness back to the spot you have chosen.

- **Continue to try to remain neutral** or unattached during your dispassionate observation. Try not to identify with an unpleasant sensation by thinking "I am in pain." If there is pain, simply note that there is pain.

- **Move your attention** to more subtle sensations. Focus on your heart beating in your chest for a few minutes. Then expand your awareness to your veins and arteries connecting to your heart and try to feel the blood pumping through them. Notice whether your heart slows down or speeds up.

- **Now focus on the general feeling** of energy moving through your body— through your arms, legs, hands, and feet. Feel energy moving around your spine, through your torso, and in your groin area. Keep your observations neutral; avoiding labeling any sensation as positive or negative. Simply experience it.

- **Next, shift your attention** to your senses. Open your eyes and focus on the small natural object you brought to the session. Using your sense of sight, observe its color, form, and markings, and whether it is smooth or rough. Try not to identify the object as "my shell" or "my flower." Simply observe it, noticing as much about it as you can.

- **Close your eyes and listen**. Pay attention to what you hear, again without labeling the sounds as pleasant or unpleasant. Simply listen carefully to sounds near and far, as well as the sound of your breath. Do this for a few minutes.

- **Open your eyes and take a bite** of the cookie. Chew carefully. Focus on the sensations on your tongue, teeth, and throat as you swallow. Try to let go of any emotions or associations you have with the cookie. If any thoughts arise, let them go and return to the simple sensations of taste.

- **Finally, focus again** on your breath for a few minutes before closing and dedicating your session.

My mindful body meditation experience

Questions to consider
How did this close awareness of my body and senses affect me?
How has this helped me become more mindful of my body in everyday life?

Date _____ Time _____

_____

_____

_____

_____

_____

_____

_____

Date _____ Time _____

_____

_____

_____

_____

_____

_____

_____

Date _____ Time _____

_____

_____

_____

_____

_____

_____

_____

_____

Date _____ Time _____

_____

_____

_____

_____

_____

_____

_____

_____

Observing my attitudes and emotions

This exercise involves choosing a personal situation or someone you know to act as your focus. By showing you how your feelings for this situation or person arose from your attitudes, it may help you to come to terms with that event or better understand the nature of your relationship.

Exercise 10 BEING MINDFUL OF MY ATTITUDES AND EMOTIONS

CD REFERENCE TRACK 1 OR TRACK 6 (OPTIONAL)

Illustration See pages 19–28 for illustrations showing sitting positions.

When to do this exercise Practice this mindfulness meditation when you would like to better understand what you are feeling or thinking about a particular person or situation.

- **Settle yourself in a comfortable** meditation sitting position (see page 42). Begin by focusing on your breath for a few minutes to calm and clear your mind.

- **Create in your mind a vivid mental image** of the situation or person you have chosen to focus on. Conjure up as much detail as possible. As you contemplate the image let your natural feelings arise and note what attitudes accompany them. It is acceptable to have a positive or negative attitude, so try not to judge yourself.

- **Now ask yourself whether** you have always held this attitude toward this person or situation. What is the origin of your attitude? What circumstance or event could change your mind? How would you feel if you never saw this person or encountered this situation again? As you explore your understanding of your attitude remember that, as with everything, it is subject to change.

- **For a few minutes try to generate** a feeling of detachment and equanimity toward this situation or person.

- **Now shift your attention** to your emotional state connected to this situation or person. How do you feel about it or him or her at this moment? Are you happy, sad, afraid, or angry? Are you experiencing a combination of emotions? Try to watch your emotional state as an observer, without identifying with it.

- **If your emotional state is pleasant**, try not to cling to it. If you are sad, try not to push it away. Remind yourself how often your emotional state shifts and how many emotions you have experienced and moved through. Meditate on the fact that all emotional states are impermanent and transitory.

- **If you have become sad** during this meditation, end by thinking of a situation or person that fills you with feelings of warmth and happiness.

My attitudes and emotions experience

Questions to consider
How did this close awareness of my attitudes and emotions affect me?
Has this exercise made me more aware of my attitudes and emotions in everyday life?
Instead of saying "I am angry," am I better able to simply note anger when it arises?

Date _____ Time _____

_____

_____

_____

_____

_____

_____

Date _____ Time _____

_____

_____

_____

_____

_____

_____

_____

Date _____ **Time** _____

_____

_____

_____

_____

_____

_____

_____

_____

Date _____ **Time** _____

_____

_____

_____

_____

_____

_____

_____

_____

Observing my mind

In this exercise you do not observe your body or emotions, but instead watch your thoughts as they glide through your consciousness, making a note of their contents. It may help to think of yourself as an anthropologist—a scientist who studies human beings and their beliefs and behavior patterns.

 Exercise 11 MINDFUL MIND
CD REFERENCE TRACK 1 OR 6 (OPTIONAL)

 Illustration See pages 19–28 for illustrations showing sitting positions.

 When to do this exercise Practice mindfulness meditation on the content of your thoughts when you wish to become conscious of patterns in your thinking or when you would like to change your life.

- **Settle yourself in a comfortable** sitting position (see page 42). Begin by simply observing your breath for a few minutes to calm and clear your mind.

- **Begin to observe your thoughts** as they enter your awareness and then disappear. While trying not to identify with or get carried away by any one thought, begin to notice the content of your thoughts. Simply observe them as an anthropologist might, from a distance, taking notes on their content. Perhaps you are thinking about meditation, or about work or your loved ones, or maybe a television show pops into your consciousness. Just notice.

- **After a few minutes**, begin to observe patterns in the content. Is there an emotional tone that repeats, such as fear or anger? Do your thoughts seem to drift to a certain subject, such as a certain person or event? Are you way in the future, planning a party or work event, or are you reliving something from this morning or your childhood? Whatever you notice, try not to judge it or yourself. Accept whatever arises.

- **Notice how by noticing your thoughts** you have become more conscious of them. This is your chance to change unhelpful patterns for more useful or compassionate ways of thinking. If you find yourself constantly worrying about the future, take a moment to breathe into the worry. Think about how in this present moment there is nothing to fear.

- **Finally, ask yourself where** these thoughts came from. Are they yours, where did they spring from, and where do they disappear to? Is this place a source of happiness? And is your consciousness unchanging or impermanent? Don't worry about finding an answer to any of these profound questions. End your meditation by dedicating your efforts to whatever seems most appropriate.

My mindful mind experience

Questions to consider
What themes did I discover in my thoughts?
What patterns seemed to recur?
Have I made efforts to change my thinking by intervening when I notice
neurotic or negative thought patterns?

Date _____ Time _____

_____

_____

_____

_____

_____

_____

Date _____ Time _____

_____

_____

_____

_____

_____

_____

Date _____ Time _____

_____

_____

_____

_____

_____

_____

_____

_____

_____

Date _____ Time _____

_____

_____

_____

_____

_____

_____

_____

_____

_____

Thinking about everything

This exercise involves choosing a costly, complex object you own to act as your focus. It allows you to explore the ties between your desires and happiness, and to start to understand the impermanent nature of everything in the universe.

 ### Exercise 12 THE TRUE NATURE OF EVERYTHING
CD REFERENCE TRACK 1 OR 6 (OPTIONAL)

 When to do this exercise Practice this meditation when you would like to explore your attachment to things, people, or experiences you have been through.

- **Begin by generating an intention** of your choosing for this meditation. Then settle yourself by meditating on your breath for a few minutes.

- **Now pick a complex object** that you own, such as a car or computer. See it in your mind's eye as vividly and solidly as you can. Then think about how that object came into being. Start by imagining the inventor or designer. Then see a large number of different factories creating the parts for your object, and the workers toiling to create them. Then see the parts gathered into one factory and your object assembled by another group of workers. Next, visualize your object on a truck, boat, or train on its way to the place where you bought it. Then see yourself interacting with a salesperson or perhaps buying it online.

- **Next see your object again clearly** and vividly. Is it in the same pristine condition as when you bought it? Does it have a few dings or nicks? Imagine how it will look in ten years time if you still have it then.

- **Now remember how much you desired** the object before you bought it. Remember how excited you were to acquire it. Is that happiness and excitement still there? How long did it take to fade?

- **Contemplate the reality** that everything is not solid and separate but is dependent on many causes and conditions; that everything is impermanent and in a constant state of flux; and that all those things outside you—whether objects, people, or experiences—cannot deliver lasting happiness. Focus again on your breath for a few minutes before closing the session.

My true nature of everything experience

Question to consider
How did this exercise affect how I feel about the objects, people, and experiences in my life?

Date _____ Time _____

_____

_____

_____

_____

_____

_____

_____

Date _____ Time _____

_____

_____

_____

_____

_____

_____

_____

MEDITATION USING SOUND

How sound affects the brain

For more than four decades, from the 1950s until his death in 2001, French doctor Alfred Tomatis devoted his life to researching auditory neurophysiology. In his research on the effects of Gregorian chant upon the brains and bodies of Benedictine monks, he discovered that the self-generated tones, elongated vowel sounds, and rhythmic breathing involved in chanting have a profound effect on mind, body, and emotions. He confirmed what meditators have known for thousands of years: that mantra recitation and chanting are highly beneficial physically, emotionally, and spiritually.

Dr Tomatis viewed the ear as the primary sensory organ affecting the brain. His invention, the "Electronic Ear," uses the filtered high-frequency sounds of Mozart, Gregorian chant, and the spoken voice to improve ear function. Centers of the Tomatis Method across the globe continue to use his techniques to treat conditions ranging from Attention Deficit Hyperactivity Disorder, chronic fatigue, and dyslexia to early childhood trauma, sexual abuse, and depression.

Therapeutic listening

According to Don Campbell, an authority on the transformational power of music, simply listening to the sounds of Gregorian chant has a beneficial effect on breathing and emotions. Researcher Pietro Modesti MD PhD, of the University of Florence, Italy, in a study conducted in 2008, found that spending just 30 minutes a day listening to rhythmically homogeneous music—anything from Western classical to Celtic to Indian music—helped lower blood pressure when combined with breathing exercises.

When it comes to listening, even cows find music therapeutic. Since the early 1990s dairy farmers in Israel, Spain, and other parts of Europe, have been exposing their heifers to the works of Mozart at milking time. As a result, farmers have seen a dramatic shift in the temperament and production of their cows, who produce from one to six more liters of milk per day, with a higher fat and protein content, than their non-Mozart listening counterparts.

Mantra meditation

In many cultures our myths of origin state that the universe came into being through sound and that the sounds we utter are the essence of being human. In *The New Testament*, St. John tells us, "In the beginning was the Word, and the Word was with God, and the Word was God." In the ancient Hindu sacred texts the *Vedas*, sound is the first sense to be created, and everything comes into being through it. When we hear or utter those sounds, we hear the essence of the created world.

What are mantras?

The most well known mantras come from the Hindu and Buddhist traditions. Here a mantra is one or more Sanskrit syllables or words that may be recited in conjunction with the practice, or *sadhana*, of meditation in honor of a particular deity. The elements of the mantra are said to embody the qualities of that deity. The word "mantra" itself combines two Sanskrit words. The first *manas* means "mind"; the second *trai* means "to protect" or "to make free from." Literally then, the word *mantra* denotes something that frees us from or protects us from the workings of the everyday mind, which we discussed on pages 50–53. This is the role of mantra meditation.

Sanskrit mantras are sounds that have specific energy vibrations that, when uttered, bring about spiritual development. The actual physical vibration of reciting the syllables of a mantra, coupled with mental intention, produces a synergistic effect for the person saying them. Mantras are known to have ancient origins and formidable power. When a skilled meditator recites a mantra as part of a *sadhana*, it helps her mind to expand and deepen. The dedicated use of mantra can also, over time, pacify the mind.

The most well known mantra in Tibetan Buddhism is *OM MANI PADME HUM*, the mantra of Avalokitesvara, the bodhisattva of compassion. Because the Dalai Lama is considered an incarnation of Avalokitesvara, his mantra is especially revered by Tibetans. In Tibet and in Nepal, the "mani" mantra, as it is known for short, is seen everywhere—carved onto

rocks by the side of the road and at the entrance to temples. It is also inserted into prayer wheels in the form of small paper scrolls. When the wheel is turned, the energy of the mantra is sent out into the universe.

What do mantras mean?

A mantra is more than the simple translation of the Sanskrit syllables. The true meaning of a mantra is the experience it creates in the person saying it, which deepens over a period of time. Those who have recited the mantra through the centuries have passed on their experiences to succeeding generations. Through thousands of years of repetition, the mantras themselves accumulate a powerful energy.

OM MANI PADME HUM is often translated as "Behold! The jewel in the lotus." *OM*, a very powerful Sanskrit mantra in itself, is said to be the sum of all the sounds in the universe. *MANI PADME* translates as "jewel in the lotus," symbolizing the two aspects of enlightenment: wisdom and compassion. *HUM* represents the limitless potential embodied in every individual being. Although the words can be translated one by one, the mantra means more than the sum of its parts and is thought to embody all the teachings of the Buddha. Taken together, the six syllables show that by uniting wisdom and compassion within yourself, you can transform your ordinary mind into the pure and loving mind of a Buddha.

How often are they repeated?

When you are reciting or chanting a mantra, the number 108 is the suggested ideal number of repetitions. This number has been considered sacred for thousands of years in India. Its origins probably lie in ancient astronomical calculations, for example, the average distance from the sun and the moon to the earth is approximately 108 times each of their respective diameters.

 Work with this exercise now Turn to Exercise 13: Mantra Meditation on page 130 and locate CD Track 5, which will teach you how to say the mantra OM MANI PADME HUM. Look carefully at the image of Avalokitesvara on the opposite page, then read through the meditation noting its main points before following the instructions.

Chanting meditation

Chanting involves speaking words or sounds or singing them in a rhythmic fashion. Chants themselves range from simple sounds on a single tone, such as the sacred Hindu and Buddhist Sanskrit syllable *OM*, to complex musical structures like the Gregorian chant that emerged from the monasteries of Europe around the 6th century. Many spiritual traditions consider chant a vehicle for spiritual development.

Chanting for spiritual development

In many traditions the repetition of a name of God or verse from a sacred text has been considered a route to spiritual growth. In the Islamic tradition *dhikr*, or remembrance of the name of God, is the devotional practice of uttering or singing the name of God or a passage from the Qu'ran many times while contemplating one's heart. The names of God may be counted on prayer beads during this practice. In the Jewish tradition a Chazanim will lead prayers in synagogue, adhering to the traditional melodies that over centuries have accrued great sanctity in themselves

and are considered capable of bringing the congregation onto a higher spiritual plane. In the Catholic church the liturgy may be chanted in Latin, a divinely revealed language whose very sounds are thought to increase reverence and help the listener to transcend the ordinary world and his ordinary mind and come into communion with Christ.

Chanting can sound very different from culture to culture. Tibetan Buddhist chant, one of the more unusual, involves a practice known as throat singing, which produces multiple pitches creating a deep-toned vibrational resonance. These low tones, which travel farther than high frequency sounds, are found in nature. For example, elephants and whales use very low tones to communicate over long distances. In order to produce their unique method of chanting, Tibetan Buddhist monks train their voices to chant two octaves below C and then employ overtones, which are heard as one note. In other words, they chant in chords. Throat singing is also practiced in Central Asia, notably by the Tuvan people, as a means

of communicating with the spirits of nature, and among the Inuit peoples of Canada and the United States.

The mantra OM

The Sanskrit syllable *OM* is pronounced as three separate syllables *A U M*. This is thought in Hinduism and Buddhism to be the sound from which all other sounds emerged—indeed, it is said to be the most sacred symbol in Sanskrit, emblematic of Brahma the creator and everything that exists. It forms part of every Hindu prayer or reading in the same way as the term *Amen* is used in Christian prayer, and is placed by Buddhists at the beginning of mantras. The meaning of this simple syllable *OM* is so profound that an entire text, the *Mandukaya Upanishad*, is given over to its explanation. *OM* encompasses the entire Hindu cosmology and everything in it. A stands for creation and Brahma the creator; U for preservation and Vishnu the preserving aspect of the divine; and M for destruction and Shiva the destroyer who disintegrates everything, reducing it to his essence so that the cycle can begin again. The curves of its written form encompass all of the

human mind and its potential for transformation: the large lower curve represents the conscious or waking state; the upper curve represents the unconscious or sleeping state; and the middle curve the dream state. The semi-circle stands for delusion, or everything holding us back from self-realization, while the dot is the state of bliss that we can achieve through meditation.

Powerful vibrations

Since the sound of *OM* is thought to be *prana* or life-force itself, the benefits that accrue when you chant this sound are almost too numerous to mention. For example, it is thought to remove worldly thoughts and the distractions of daily life, helping you to stay focused on your spiritual priorities. It focuses and calms the mind and can be a powerful healing tonic, filling you with energy and vitality. It can also help to counter chronic low energy and depression. You don't have to chant *OM* only when sitting to meditate; make it part of your daily life, too, by chanting for example when walking to work, singing a toddler to sleep, or whenever you feel jaded or out of sorts.

 Work with this exercise now Turn to Exercise 14: Chanting OM on page 134. Read through the meditation, noting its main points, then follow the instructions.

Meditation using music

Music may be one of the oldest of human art forms. It is not difficult to imagine our ancestors keeping rhythm by hitting a stick on a hollow log or playing a tune on a hand-carved flute. And of course it is easy to imagine a solo voice ringing out over the pristine savannah, or a group singing around the night fire. You may already be a singer or a musician yourself, and know just how much beauty and stimulation music can provide.

Even though it can be recorded, music is always created in the present moment and then gone. It reverberates in the air in the form of invisible sound waves and is by nature impermanent. That sound at that moment can never be repeated in exactly the same way. Even if you are listening to a recording, your experience listening in one moment is unique. The next time you listen you will have a different experience.

Music is vibration, and it synchronizes and harmonizes with the vibration of our bodies, our minds, and the universe. It can sometimes seem mysterious; a reflection of something beyond our ordinary world. Music can transport us, at least for a moment, to another way of being. It can be an inspiration and an invitation to a more conscious way of living—one that is focused on the present.

Unimagined sounds

Unfamiliar music, or music from other cultures, is an excellent focus for meditation. For example, various forms of world music may provide you with the experience of new rhythms, harmonies, melodies, and scales. Try listening to African drums, the Indian sitar, Spanish guitar, the Japanese Zen shakuhachi flute, or any other music that sounds new to your ear. When you meditate on music, focus on the sounds as you would your breath. Let your body and mind function as an expanded ear; let go of all thoughts and put your complete attention on each note. Follow the melodies and chords and the various instruments that may be new and unfamiliar without judging them. Let the sounds enter you and take you over for the duration of your meditation session.

 **Work with this exercise now** Turn to Exercise 15: Meditation with Music on page 138. Read through the exercise and note the main points of the instructions, then begin the meditation.

Meditation with nature sounds

The opportunities to listen to the sounds of nature are endless. Even in a large city birds, crickets, and other insects chirp and buzz if you take the time to listen. Then there is the sound of rain and wind, lightning and thunder, or rustling leaves. Meditating on the sounds of nature helps you to pay attention to aspects of the world you do not ordinarily hear. It grounds and connects you to the rest of the living universe—an experience that can be inspiring, humbling, and healing.

Of all the sounds in nature, the sound of the ocean is one of the most affecting and moving. Its salty waters symbolize life itself. The ocean breathes as you breathe, its waves inhaling and exhaling, drawing in and pulling out against the shore. Its tides and the moon are intimately connected. It is vast, covering a large portion of the earth, and much of its depths are yet to be explored and discovered. Your consciousness and spiritual potential is as vast as the ocean, and through meditation you can plumb its depths.

Limitless depths

The ocean metaphor is a favorite of Tibetan Buddhists, whose spiritual and temporal leader's name, the Dalai Lama, means "Ocean of Wisdom." The great leader of India, Mahatma Gandhi, also referred to the need to merge himself in and identify with "this limitless ocean of life" in order to realize the truth. Contemplating the sounds of the ocean—using it as a focus of meditation—allows you to recognize the limitless potential of your own mind, and to escape narrow ideas and restricted ways of thinking. Ninety-five percent of the vast oceans of the earth remain a mystery to humankind, and are yet to be explored. As such, the ocean provides you with a dynamic symbol for the unexplored parts of yourself—your psyche, your mind, and your unconscious. It challenges you to be fearless and go deep rather than stay on the surface of life. It allows you to imagine your ability to expand beyond what you are to what you can be.

 **Work with this exercise now** Turn to Exercise 16: Meditating on the Sound of the Ocean on page 142 and locate CD Track 6. Find a place indoors where you can sit comfortably and have a CD player nearby. Read through the meditation noting its main points, then follow the instructions.

SOUND MEDITATION
EXERCISES

For thousands of years meditation masters have recognized
and used the power of the voice and sound in their
meditation practice. The following exercises will provide you
with ways to bring the healing and transformative aspects of
sound into your meditation practice.

Meditating on a mantra

This exercise introduces you to the power of reciting an age-old mantra. Listen to the CD well to tune your ear to the sounds of the different Sanskrit syllables before you start to chant. Although it is not necessary, a Buddhist rosary or *mala* is useful to help you keep count of the repetitions in this exercise.

Exercise 13 MANTRA MEDITATION

CD REFERENCE TRACK 5

 **Illustration** See pages 19–28 for illustrations showing sitting positions. See page 119 for an illustration of Avalokitesvara.

 **When to do this exercise** Practice this meditation when you wish to connect with the energy of wisdom and compassion in yourself and in the universe, and to develop your own potential for growing those aspects of yourself.

- **Choose a seated meditation posture** (see page 42) and begin by setting your intention for this meditation: that you will grow in wisdom and compassion. Then meditate on your breath for a few minutes.

- **Play CD Track 5 and listen** to the pronunciation of the mantra OM MANI PADME HUM. Visualize the Buddhist bodhisattva of compassion Avalokitesvara seated cross-legged in front of you on a lotus cushion. Look at the image of him on page 119. He is pure white in color and has four arms. With two of his hands he clasps a jewel between his palms, which are touching in a gesture of prayer. The other two hands are upraised to the right and left, one holding a string of crystal beads symbolic of contemplation, the other a lotus, signifying spiritual perfection.

- **Holding the picture** of Avalokitesvara in your mind, begin to recite the mantra out loud. Then recite it more softly. Finally, recite it with just your lips moving. Try to utter the mantra at least 108 times, counting on your fingers or on the beads of a *mala*.

- **As you recite the mantra** think of its translation, "Behold! The jewel in the lotus." This phrase represents the two aspects of enlightenment—wisdom and compassion—and the union of those ideals within you. It also represents your limitless potential as a human being.

- **When you are ready** to close your meditation, end the recitation and dedicate your practice to your own spiritual development.

My mantra meditation experience

Questions to consider
What effects did the visualization and mantra recitation have on my body?
What effects did the visualization and mantra recitation have on my mind?

Date _____ Time _____

_____

_____

_____

_____

_____

_____

_____

Date _____ Time _____

_____

_____

_____

_____

_____

_____

_____

Date _____ Time _____

_____

_____

_____

_____

_____

_____

_____

_____

_____

_____

Date _____ Time _____

_____

_____

_____

_____

_____

_____

_____

_____

_____

_____

Using the mantra OM

As you practice chanting this mantra, try to remember that the sacred sound *OM* is considered to be the sum of all the sounds in the universe. And so by making this sound you connect yourself to everything that is. Allow yourself to feel energized and renewed as you recite *OM*, which has been chanted for thousands of years by millions before you.

 ## Exercise 14 CHANTING OM
CD REFERENCE TRACK 1 OR TRACK 6 (OPTIONAL)

 Illustration See pages 19–28 for illustrations showing sitting positions.

 When to do this exercise Chant OM whenever you are stressed and/or feel low in energy. To avoid feeling self-conscious or attracting unwanted attention, chant in a place where you can be alone and undisturbed.

- **Find a spot where you can** be alone and undisturbed. Choose a comfortable meditation sitting position (see page 42) and take a few deep belly breaths. Then focus on your breath for a few minutes until you feel mentally calm and physically relaxed.

- **Begin slowly by breathing in** and then exhaling a single note. Once you find a tone you feel comfortable with, chant the syllable OM repeatedly on each out-breath.

- **Sound out the syllable** in three parts: A — U — M. Say "Ahhhhh" as your breath releases, "ooooouuhh" to express your feelings of calm and peace, and "mmmmm" as you end the mantra by closing your lips. For a few minutes focus on nothing but the sound itself and the vibrations it generates in your body.

- **Now extend the OM**, making it slower, longer, and lower. See if you can make the chant come from way down in your throat and let it resonate throughout every part of your body. Concentrate on the space between your eyebrows —your "third eye"—as you try to feel the pure, all-pervading light and consciousness of the universe vibrating within you. Let every part of your body resonate with these thoughts.

- **Chant the syllable 108 times** in total. When you complete your chanting, sit quietly and focus on your breath. When you are ready, dedicate your meditation to whatever seems most appropriate.

My chanting OM experience

Questions to consider
What effect did chanting OM have on my body?
What effect did chanting OM have on my mind?
Did chanting stir up any emotions for me?

Date _____ Time _____

_____
_____
_____
_____
_____
_____
_____

Date _____ Time _____

_____
_____
_____
_____
_____
_____
_____

Date _____ Time _____

_____

_____

_____

_____

_____

_____

_____

_____

_____

Date _____ Time _____

_____

_____

_____

_____

_____

_____

_____

_____

_____

Using music in my meditation

For this exercise choose a piece of music that is new and unfamiliar. It can be of any genre, but it is best to choose an instrumental track so that you can focus on the music itself without getting caught up in the lyrics. The only exception would be a song or a chant in a language that is foreign to you. If you like classical music, by all means listen to it, but choose a composer, a piece of music, an era, or musical instrument you are not familiar with.

Exercise 15 MEDITATION WITH MUSIC

 **Illustration** See pages 18–25 for illustrations showing sitting positions.

 **When to do this exercise** Meditate on music as a way of deepening your understanding of the form and structure of music, and to expand your sense of yourself as part of a larger vibrational universe.

- **Choose a comfortable sitting meditation posture** (see page 42) or lie on your back. Set up your music player within reach. Take three deep belly breaths (see page 38) then simply focus on your breath for a few minutes until you feel relaxed and centered. Choose an intention for this meditation that feels right to you.

- **Now play the music you have chosen** and close your eyes. Listen as if you are a Martian who has never heard music before. Focus completely on the sound of the music and nothing else. Listen to each note and the trajectory of each instrument. If thoughts intervene, simply return to the sound as you would your breath. Notice how the music affects your breath.

- **Listen to one or more tracks**, or for as long as you like, while remaining in a meditative state.

- **When you are ready** to end your session, focus on your breath for a few minutes then dedicate your meditation in whichever way seems appropriate.

My music meditation experience

Questions to consider
How did this exercise affect my appreciation of sound?
How did this exercise affect my understanding of music?

Date _____ Time _____

_____

_____

_____

_____

_____

_____

Date _____ Time _____

_____

_____

_____

_____

_____

_____

Date _____ Time _____

_____

_____

_____

_____

_____

_____

_____

Date _____ Time _____

_____

_____

_____

_____

_____

_____

_____

Using ocean sounds

This meditation marries your powers of visualization to the relaxing and cleansing potential of the sounds of the sea on CD Track 6. You might also like to use this track during other meditations, too, or, if you are experiencing insomnia, use it to relax your mind and lull your body into sleep.

Exercise 16 MEDITATING ON THE SOUND OF THE OCEAN CD REFERENCE TRACK 6

Illustration See pages 19–28 for illustrations showing meditation sitting positions.

When to do this exercise Practice this meditation when you want to relieve stress, when you feel stuck or hemmed in by a situation or a relationship, when you are looking for creative inspiration, or when you want to heal from an illness.

• **Choose a sitting meditation posture** (see page 42) or lie on your back. Make sure the CD player is within reach. Breathe deeply for a few breaths and then breathe normally. Focus on your breath for several minutes until you feel calm and present. Notice any areas of your body that are tense and consciously relax them by breathing into them.

- **Visualize yourself beside the ocean**, alone with no one else in sight. Imagine you are sitting on a beach looking out at the water. Notice its many shades of blue, gray, green, and white. Feel yourself there. Notice the texture of the sand, the salty tang in the air, and the few white clouds in the sky. Feel the warmth of the sun and the perfect temperature on your skin. When you are ready, turn on Track 6 on the CD player and listen to the sounds of the ocean.

- **While maintaining the feeling** that you are actually at the seaside, shift your focus to the sounds of the ocean. Let the sounds wash over you and cleanse away any worries or fears that may be lurking in the background of your mind. Let the ocean sounds heal any illness or medical condition that you may have. Hear the ocean breathing with you as you breathe. Listen to its waves inhaling and exhaling, drawing in and pulling out against the shore.

- **Contemplate the thought** that your consciousness and spiritual potential is as vast as the ocean, and that through meditation you can reach down and sample its depths.

- **When the track ends**, finish your meditation, or play the track again if you would like to continue.

My ocean meditation experience

Questions to consider
How did I feel before and after meditating on the sounds of the ocean?
Did meditating on the sounds of the ocean lead to any insights about my
current situation in life?

Date _____ Time _____

_____
_____
_____
_____
_____
_____

Date _____ Time _____

_____
_____
_____
_____
_____
_____

MEDITATION THROUGH VISUALIZATION

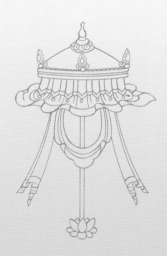

How visualization affects the brain

The use of images and visualization has been an important aspect of various forms of meditation for thousands of years. The sense of sight combined with the ability of the brain to generate visual images on its own has been a powerful tool for spiritual transformation. Hindus, Buddhists, and many other spiritual practitioners have made extensive use of visualization in their meditation practice. External images—such as pictures of the Buddha or Christ, or spiritual diagrams such as Hindu yantras, Buddhist mandalas, or the Christian rose windows of Gothic cathedrals—have been used extensively as aids for prayer and meditation.

Why it works

Research shows that there is a strong scientific basis for how and why imagery and visualization enhance meditation and spiritual development. The left and right hemispheres of the brain function in different ways. The left is the domain of serial, linear information; the right of spatial knowledge and creativity. If you tell your left brain something in a thousand words, it will methodically process the information for you. But draw it a picture, and your right brain will respond with much deeper interest and attention. Images can symbolize and contain a vast amount of information. For example, rose windows in churches use image, color, and symbolism to teach worshippers about the mysteries of Christ while providing an object of contemplation.

It is now well known that we stimulate the same areas of the brain when visualizing an action as when actually performing that action. For example, when you visualize lifting your left foot you stimulate the same part of your brain that is activated when you actually lift your left foot. When you visualize yourself as a compassionate Buddha therefore, the areas of your brain associated with feeling and compassion become more active too.

Yantras and meditation

Yantras are drawings or paintings used as an aid for meditation in the Hindu tantric tradition. They are an ancient spiritual technology for discovering cosmic and spiritual truths. As for the word *mantra* (see pages 116–117), the Sanskrit derivation of the term yantra provide clues to how it works. The word translates as a mechanical device or instrument for restraining something, or a prop or support, suggesting that in one image, the *yantra* represents both the act of subduing the distractions and delusions of the body and mind, and the way to gain liberation from the worldly. A yantra shows in visual form the movement away from ordinary life and toward union with universal consciousness and enlightenment.

Like mandalas, yantras are two-dimensional, but represent the three-dimensional world we currently inhabit as well as the multidimensions of ultimate reality in the Hindu tradition. Their complex geometric patterns simultaneously embody the energetic patterns of the subtle body of the practitioner and of the multidimensional universe. This makes them power diagrams. For instance a triangle pointing upward represents masculine, out-going energy and the god Shiva (who stands for the universal masculine principle), while a downward-pointing triangle carries feminine qualities of creativity and introspection and the goddess Shakti (the universal female principle). Allowing the eye to gaze upon these shapes therefore transports the viewer on a complex interior journey as well as uniting him or her with the Hindu cosmos.

Dynamics of yantra meditation

Yantras are usually associated with the energies of particular deities. After consecrating the yantra, the adept often visualizes the deity and the yantra simultaneously, building up the image of the deity in his or her mind. Then he or she begins the yantra

meditation by focusing on the periphery, the beginning of the journey to the center. The symmetry of the diagram naturally draws attention toward the central point, or *bindu* as circuit-by-circuit, the person meditating works his or her way to the center.

The symbols contained in the yantra point to negative mental patterns or physical activities that must be transformed in the pursuit of liberation. The yantra meditation progresses from the gross to the subtle along ascending planes of consciousness. When the person meditating reaches the center of the yantra, the deity disappears and merges with the *bindu* of the yantra, which then merges with the meditator's third eye. The *bindu* is experienced as all that is, and the adept and the symbol merge to become one. The journey from the periphery to the center of the yantra

—to the primordial source represented by the central point—is only a few inches, but psychologically the journey is a vast distance and takes a lifetime of discipline.

Meditation on the Shri yantra

The Shri yantra is considered to be one of the greatest yantras, comprised of a central white *bindu* point and a series of radiating red triangles surrounded by two rings of lotus petals and a square temple shape with four "doors" or entry points. The *bindu* sits within a downward-pointing red triangle which contains the power of feminine energy, and from this radiate nine interlocking red and white triangles; four white "male" and four red "female" energies. The yantra broadens out into 43 small triangles that in their interconnection represent divine energy and the potent union of masculine and feminine in the universe.

 Work with this exercise now First copy and enlarge the yantra opposite, then turn to Exercise 17: Meditation on the Shri Yantra. You can choose to work with a more complex guided version of this meditation or a simpler one.

I'm not there yet If the complex version of the meditation seems too difficult for you, choose the simpler one.

Mandalas and meditation

As a symbol of nature, the mandala reflects the symmetry of all natural forms. Plants, animals, crystals, electrons in their orbits and cells in their membranes—all are made up of circular structures. As a symbol of time, the mandala reminds us of natural cycles, such as the wheel of the year and the recurring progression of days and seasons. It expresses past, present, and future simultaneously. As a symbol of culture, the mandala suggests the circle of community. It reminds us that we long for the warmth, support, and protection of the center and fear being marginalized at the periphery. As a symbol of human wholeness and well-being, the mandala describes the experience of integration—our positive and negative aspects are contained and supported by the boundary of our sense of self.

The universe as mandala

Though we may never really know how the universe began, human beings throughout time have intuitively used a dot at the center of a circle to depict the origin of all reality. Hindus call this dot the *bindu*, or sacred point, the source from which everything that exists emanates. The ancient peoples who worshipped the Great Goddess called the universe "the Great Round" and depicted its center as the *ompholos* or navel of the world. Tibetan Buddhist meditators place a divine being in the center of their mandalas. They then dissolve their everyday world of appearances and mentally arise in the form of a deity surrounded by a perfect mandala universe—a kind of sacred roleplay that powers their drive toward spiritual attainment. Even today, the Big Bang theory of modern physics proposes that the universe came into being—and is still expanding—from an explosion of a single primeval atom. Perhaps all mandalas, both human-made and natural, reflect the expansion of the universe from an original, primeval point.

153

As a symbol of the universe, the mandala helps us to contemplate life's big questions. When we meditate on a mandala we are invited to focus on questions concerning the mysteries of the universe as well as our own lives, such as:

- Where did we come from, and where are we going?
- Did the universe have a beginning, and does it have an end?
- Where *is* the center of the universe, or is there one?

The mandala as spiritual journey

Mandalas symbolize the presence of the sacred in our mundane realm. Mathematicians tell us that the point at the center of a circle is dimensionless.

This "essence" at the center is contained within a limited space bounded by a circumference. So the mandala as symbol can show us the boundless universe that lies at the heart of our small everyday world.

By moving toward and meditating on the essence at the center of a mandala, you come to understand the sacred nature of all reality. Coming back from the center into everyday reality, you perceive simultaneously the mundane and the sacred. You experience yourself and everything in your environment as essentially "one." As The Buddha said (as recorded in the Heart Sutra), "Form is the essence and essence is the form" or as Christ expressed in a similar idea, "the Kingdom of God is within you."

 Work with this exercise now First copy and enlarge the mandala on the opposite page, then turn to Exercise 18: Mandala Meditation on page 166 and follow the instructions.

Using visualization

Visualization is an aspect of many forms of meditation and a powerful technique for personal transformation. It gives us a taste of the spiritual life in a way that words never can. Instead of just hearing about the wisdom teachings of various traditions, visualization allows us to live them out in our minds. This imaginative participation in spiritual experience is what makes it such an effective tool for transformation.

Visualization allows us to imagine the person we want to become and the qualities we want to embody. It permits us to feel the love and compassion of our higher power, however we conceive it. Through visualization we can also stimulate areas of the brain that help our bodies to heal. For example, athletes practice by visualizing running a race or playing a game. As they do so, areas of the brain fire as if the person visualizing were actually leading the race or winning the game. This works in terms of health, too. Through visualization, we can give our brains messages to heal our bodies and cells. By actually seeing ourselves, in the mind's eye, whole and healed and the recipient of the universe's love and compassion, we can hasten healing. Through visualization we can help relieve suffering, end obsessions and addictions, and live a more positive and productive life.

Visualization from emptiness

One of the best techniques for beginning a visualization meditation is to imagine a vast expanse of blue sky, totally clear and luminous and stretching out endlessly in all directions. This gives us a blank slate and a way to enter the meditative state. For the moment, when we step into this space nothing can bother us. We can let go of our worries and problems, our grasping and irritation, and just relax. As we visualize this bright, peaceful, and spacious sky our mind takes on those qualities. There is tremendous freedom in the sky and it reminds us that the mind in its natural state is equally vast, free, calm, and peaceful.

The blue sky also reminds us that the nature of everything is impermanence. Everything can change, transform, and

develop—including us. By consciously directing our thoughts and behavior we can move the flow of change in a positive way, transforming ourselves into the person we want to be. Out of the blue sky, which is empty of anything fixed, we can begin to build a vision of healing and inspiration.

Visualization and emotion

When we learned about mindfulness meditation on pages 82–96, we explored mindfulness of our emotions and how they are often bound up with attachment or aversion. Our emotions can cause pain and suffering for ourselves and others, and we explored the ways in which they do this. Yet emotion is a part of our human nature. We are feeling creatures and positive feelings enhance our lives and help us communicate with others. Emotion can also enhance and strengthen our visualization. When you practice the following visualization exercise, invite and encourage any positive emotions that may arise. This visualization uses the Buddha as its focus, but you do not have to be a Buddhist to practice or benefit from it.

 Work with this exercise now Turn to Exercise 19: Visualizing the Buddha on page 170 and then follow the guided instructions on Track 8 of the CD.

Nature-watching

Meditation on the visual aspects of nature can help to realign you with some of the deepest roots of your being. Our ancient ancestors spent much of their time looking at nature in order to survive, and graced us with their exquisite cave paintings of animals as a record of their keen observation. The paintings express great affection and joy for the beauty of the animal world as well as respect and gratitude for the role these creatures play in the survival of mankind. Our ancestors' ability to observe minute variations of color, texture, movement, and form in nature had a direct connection to whether they lived or died. That snake phobias are common today when snakes are rarely a threat in daily life is a reminder that some primitive part of the human brain learned to be afraid at the sight of these creatures.

Reconnecting with nature through the sense of sight reconnects us with the beauty we so often miss by spending much of the day indoors. If you look closely at a blue-green iridescent moth or the veins in a leaf up close, examine the rough bark of a tree, or catch a blur of red fur out of the corner of your eye, you may be both delighted and shocked. Making the transition from television and computer screens to the reality of nature can be an emotionally moving experience, like coming home after being gone for decades.

Take your time

It can take time to begin to see nature clearly and deeply. Making nature-watching a meditative practice can hasten that experience. Go on nature walks alone to begin to attune your visual attention so that it is receptive and open-ended. Then you begin to receive into your awareness everything around you. As with breath meditation, any time you find yourself thinking about something else, simply bring your awareness back to the natural world around you.

Work with this exercise now Turn to Exercise 20: Seeing Nature on page 174. Read through the instructions and then follow the meditation, contemplating the points you choose to work with.

VISUALIZATION EXERCISES

The exercises in this section will introduce you to the power imagery has when used in a meditation practice, whether you are contemplating a man-made object such as a mandala or the beauty of the natural world.

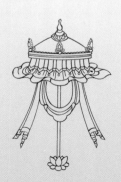

Meditating with a yantra

Before starting this meditation, make a copy of the yantra on page 150, enlarging it so that you can clearly see it from an arm's distance away. Pin it up at eye level where you sit to meditate. There are two ways to meditate using the yantra. The first is to meditate on the specific symbols and forms within the yantra, moving from the outside inward. To do this, listen to the guided meditation on CD track 7. The second method is simpler: just gaze on the yantra until you feel a sense of resonance with it, using the instructions given here.

 Exercise 17 MEDITATION ON THE SHRI YANTRA
CD REFERENCE TRACK 7 (TO FOLLOW THE SCRIPT, TURN TO PAGE 246)

Illustration See pages 19–28 for illustrations showing sitting positions. You will find the illustration of the yantra on page 150.

When to do this exercise Try this when you would like to experiment with imagery in your meditation practice or want to explore a Hindu method of meditation.

- **Hang the enlarged copy of the yantra** on a wall, placing its central point, or *bindu* at eye level. Sit on a cushion or chair maintaining a straight spine (see page 42). Let your breath flow normally.

- **Generate the aspiration** to experience the energies of expanded consciousness as you gaze on this yantra. Ask that you be guided to experience the oneness of the universe.

- **Look into the center of the yantra**, trying to blink as rarely as possible. Instead of looking at the details of the yantra, keep your eyes focused on the center and observe the whole image at once. When thoughts arise, simply bring your focus back to the yantra.

- **Continue gazing at the yantra** for 15 minutes. When you end your meditation, dedicate the fruits of your practice to your higher power or your own enlightenment. Repeat the meditation daily for at least a week.

My yantra meditation experience

Question to consider
How did meditating on the yantra affect my sense of myself?

Date _____ Time _____

_____
_____
_____
_____
_____
_____
_____

Date _____ Time _____

_____
_____
_____
_____
_____
_____
_____

Date _____ Time _____

_____

_____

_____

_____

_____

_____

_____

_____

Date _____ Time _____

_____

_____

_____

_____

_____

_____

_____

_____

Meditating with a mandala

Meditating on the outline of a mandala while coloring it in is an interesting, contemporary method of working with mandalas. The act of coloring has a meditative quality that helps concentrate the mind, allowing unconscious thoughts and emotions to surface. This can be a good way to explore a problem or ask a question to which you would like an answer. Before starting this meditation, make a copy and enlarge the mandala on page 155. You will also need a set of colored pencils or marker pens.

 ### Exercise 18 MANDALA MEDITATION
CD REFERENCE TRACK 1 OR TRACK 6 (OPTIONAL)

 Illustration You will find the illustration of the mandala on page 155.

 When to do this exercise Try this when you want to experiment with imagery in your meditation, using the mandala as your focus.

- **Prepare your materials** by gathering together the enlarged copy of the mandala and your colored pencils or markers. Then find a place where you can be alone and sit undisturbed.

- **Sit and focus on your breath** for a few minutes to center and calm your mind. Now decide on the problem you wish to explore or the question you wish to ask. Write it down in brief on the back of the mandala. Alternatively, simply open yourself to whatever comes up as you color the mandala.

- **Arrange your pencils or markers** so you can see all of them. Avoid thinking about the colors and simply pick one that you are drawn to. Begin coloring, working from the outside in and generally completing each circuit or ring before moving inward. Work as slowly or as fast as you prefer.

- **Whether you are focusing on a problem** or simply allowing whatever comes up to present itself, only focus on your breath as you color. If thoughts arise, simply let them emerge, linger, and disappear as you return to your coloring and your breath.

- **After completing your mandala** turn the page to write about your experience.

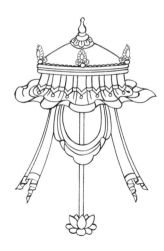

My mandala meditation experience

Questions to consider
If I had a specific problem or question, did coloring the mandala bring me any insight?
What feelings or thoughts emerged as I reached the center of the mandala?

Date _____ Time _____

_____

_____

_____

_____

_____

_____

Date _____ Time _____

_____

_____

_____

_____

_____

_____

Date _____ Time _____

_____

_____

_____

_____

_____

_____

_____

Date _____ Time _____

_____

_____

_____

_____

_____

_____

_____

_____

Working with visualization

This visualization is a meditation on Buddha Shakyamuni, the founder of Buddhism. You do not have to be a Buddhist to meditate on the Buddha, or give up your chosen religion, and if you prefer, you may substitute another higher power, such as God the Father or Jesus Christ, Mohammad, the Virgin Mary, a saint, or any other holy person or being who inspires you.

 ### Exercise 19 VISUALIZING THE BUDDHA
CD REFERENCE TRACK 8 (TO FOLLOW THE SCRIPT, TURN TO PAGE 248)

Illustration See pages 19–28 for illustrations showing sitting positions. For an illustration of Buddha Shakyamuni, turn to page 147.

When to do this exercise Try this meditation whenever you would like to explore the power of visualization in meditation practice and in your daily life.

- **Sit quietly in a meditation position** (see page 42) and close your eyes. If you have trouble creating a mental visual image or "seeing" in your mind's eye, follow these steps before beginning the guided meditation on CD Track 8. If you feel comfortable, turn on the track now and follow its instructions instead.

- **Keeping your eyes closed** bring to mind a very familiar scene, such as your living room. Mentally stand in the doorway and look around the room, starting from your right. Try to see in your mind's eye the furniture and other objects in the room.

- **Moving your inner gaze** slowly, take in every detail. See the color and texture of the fabrics on the furniture, the carpet, or the drapes. Notice the pictures on the wall, the content of the images and the nature of the frames. Observe the lamps, the objects on the coffee table, your TV, and anything else in the room. Slowly move around the room leaving nothing unnoticed until you return to the doorway where you are standing.

- **Now imagine yourself walking** into the room and sitting down. Look back at the doorway from where you are sitting. See it as clearly as you can. When you are ready, stop this practice visualization, turn on CD Track 8, and follow the guided meditation.

My visualizing the Buddha experience

Questions to consider

How did visualizing a loving, compassionate higher power feel to me?

Did I experience any changes in my body or mental state after this meditation?

Date _____ Time _____

_____

_____

_____

_____

_____

_____

_____

Date _____ Time _____

_____

_____

_____

_____

_____

_____

_____

Date _____ Time _____

_____

_____

_____

_____

_____

_____

_____

_____

Date _____ Time _____

_____

_____

_____

_____

_____

_____

_____

_____

Meditating with nature

To practice this meditation you will need to find a place in nature, perhaps a park, beach, or wildlife reserve, where you can sit and be alone. If you need something to sit on, such as a blanket or folding chair, take it with you. Bring this book along, too, so you can review the meditation.

Exercise 20 SEEING NATURE

 **Illustration** See pages 19–28 for illustrations showing meditation sitting positions.

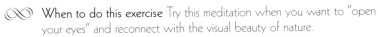 **When to do this exercise** Try this meditation when you want to "open your eyes" and reconnect with the visual beauty of nature.

- **Sit in your chosen spot in nature**, making sure that it is somewhere you will not be disturbed. Sit and just observe, focusing on your breath. As each detail in your natural setting comes into awareness, add it to what you are already conscious of.

- **Slowly widen the range of your focus**, letting nature in. Allow the beauty around you to enter your visual consciousness. Breathe it in with your eyes. Let the colors and patterns fill your mind. Try not to think or judge, just let your visual field fill with nature.

- **Find one object you would like** to spend some time with and place your entire attention on it. It could be a leaf, a flower, or an insect. Examine it intently; any time your mind wanders or thoughts arise, simply return to seeing. Try not to analyze or think about what you are looking at, and simply see what is. Notice everything you can about your object—its colors, form, and detail. When you feel you have seen everything there is to see, look again and go deeper.

- **Now shift your perception** back to the entire natural space around you. Notice how the objects in your field of vision relate to each other. Perhaps the insects are feeding on a dead tree stump, a leaf is decaying and fertilizing the forest floor, or a deer is peering at you from behind the trees, her fur blending with the color of the tree trunks. Begin to see subtle motion in stillness.

- **Return your awareness** to the entire space within your vision. Sit for a few minutes focusing on your breath. Express gratitude for the privilege and mystery of being here on earth. Then end your meditation.

My seeing nature experience

Question to consider
How did this exercise change my experience of nature?

Date _____ Time _____

_____
_____
_____
_____
_____
_____
_____

Date _____ Time _____

_____
_____
_____
_____
_____
_____
_____

MEDITATION
THROUGH
MOVEMENT

How body and mind work together

The ancient healthcare systems of India and China, Tibet, and the Islamic world have always taught that mind and body are indivisible: that what affects the mind will affect the body, and that only when the mind is calm and clear can the body enjoy good health. Unfortunately, in the West conventional allopathic medicine has, until recently, preferred to think of the body and mind as separate entities, choosing to focus on and treat apparently unrelated symptoms rather than in a more holistic way.

However, echoing ancient Eastern wisdom, molecular biologist Dr. Candice Pert states that at the molecular level, there is no distinction between mind and body in her groundbreaking 1999 book *Molecules of Emotion: the science behind mind-body medicine*. According to Dr. Pert, every thought we have influences millions of atoms, molecules, and cells throughout the body; it literally becomes the body. And every change in the body is accompanied by a comparable change in our mental and emotional state, whether we are conscious of it or not. Communication is carried out by neuropeptides and their receptors—Dr. Pert calls them "the biochemicals of emotions"—which transport messages in the vast network that links body and mind.

Meditation in action

When you practice moving meditations such as walking meditation, tai chi, chi kung, and yoga, you work directly with the mind-body connection. For example, in tai chi you learn to focus on each motion and become aware of the processes at work in both your body and mind, so that the mind is stilled and every movement is poised. When practicing walking meditation, you coordinate your breath with your movement as you meditate. In chi kung, you work with *chi* energy, which has a powerful effect on both body and mind. Yoga, first conceived as an aspect of meditation rather than a physical health practice, puts you in touch with your body as a vehicle for enlightenment.

Meditative walking

In Japanese Zen Buddhism, students sit for long periods in meditation, a practice known as *zazen*. But between periods of sitting, they engage in shorter periods of *kinhin*, or walking meditation. This allows the body to move, restoring blood flow and making it possible to sit comfortably for another period of *zazen*, but preserves the stillness of the meditative mental state. In order to maintain the alertness of the sitting practice, students hold their arms in a particular way: the elbows point outward and the left hand makes a fist; the right palm rests on top. The forward movement is very, very slow, with only a half-step taken with each breath. When the practice ends, practitioners bring both feet together and make a short bow before sitting again for *zazen*. If you are doing walking meditation on your own, choose a space, inside or outside, without obstacles. A long hall or room, a backyard, or a path in a park is a good choice; just make sure you can walk in a straight line.

Putting it into practice

Walking meditation is an opportunity to put into practice all your resolutions to slow down and pay attention to the present. In ordinary life we are often distracted by anxieties and fears, memories of the past and plans for the future, so our walking is not relaxed. With walking meditation, you can relax and experience each step in the moment. There is nowhere to arrive and you are not trying to accomplish a goal. At first, you may feel awkward walking very slowly, and the short steps and arm position might throw you off balance rather, but after a little practice you will be able to enjoy walking with a fine focus and complete relaxation. The important thing is not to try too hard, but instead to sense the tiny shifts in weight and forward motion, giving in to the gift of movement.

In the following exercise, you will be introduced to walking meditation. Remember to walk extremely slowly and to coordinate your steps with your breath. Keep your spine as straight as bamboo, and position your nose over your navel and your ears over your shoulders. Keep your head level but focus your eyes on the ground where you will next place your foot. Consciously feel the connection between your foot and the earth.

Work with this exercise now Turn to Exercise 21: Walking Meditation on page 194 and follow the instructions.

Tai chi meditation

The term Tai Chi Chuan can be translated as "Supreme Ultimate Force" or, more literally, "Supreme Ultimate Fist." "Supreme ultimate" refers to the Chinese concept of Yin and Yang, the idea of a dynamic duality that pervades all things. Yin and Yang manifest in the duality of male and female, active and passive, dark and light, forceful and yielding, and sun and moon. The symbol of tai chi is the dark/light circular Yin Yang symbol. The "Force" refers to the martial aspect of tai chi chuan. The practice of tai chi chuan, or tai chi consists of learning a sequence of movements called a form. Many of these movements are derived from the martial arts, and are actually kicks, punches, strikes, and blocks. However, in tai chi, these movements are performed in graceful slow motion, with smooth, seamless transitions.

In Beijing and other parts of China, it is common for people to gather in open spaces, such as public squares, early in the morning to practice tai chi. Although each individual is absorbed in his or her own meditation in motion and does not focus on the actions of the neighbors, they often appear to be moving in unison. Similar scenes are becoming familiar in parks and colleges in the West, as tai chi gains popularity there.

For most tai chi enthusiasts, the focus is not on martial arts but on health, longevity, and the meditative qualities of the practice. Most find it a great stress reliever and it can be a wonderful practice for chronic conditions, such as arthritis or high blood pressure. One of the purposes of tai chi is to encourage the circulation of *chi* or vital energy within the body, thus enhancing health and vitality. Practicing the form also helps with balance, spinal alignment, and motor control, and tai chi is especially helpful for the elderly in preventing falls. It can help foster rhythm and grace in everyday movement, and improve posture. Areas of the body that were chronically tense can be released. As a meditative practice, tai chi can help calm the body and mind and open the practitioner to deeper spiritual realization.

Tai chi's Taoist roots

The roots of tai chi lie in the Chinese philosophy of Taoism, a mystical Chinese tradition associated with the scholar Lao Tsu, who lived in the 6th century BCE. He is perhaps best known as the author of the *Tao Te Ching*. Lao Tsu promoted a calm, reflective, mystical, and individualistic view of the world that relied on the beauty and tranquility of nature. In China today, tai chi is almost exclusively practiced outside in nature, and is still associated with the calm and serene, yielding philosophy of Taoism.

Forms of tai chi

Today, there are many schools of tai chi in China and around the world and the forms vary, some having as few as

183

thirteen and others hundreds of movements. Yang, Wu, and Chen styles are the most well known, all named after the families that created them. The Short Yang Style Form is the easiest form of tai chi to learn and the most accessible to people of all ages and physical abilities. The exercise on pages 198–199 is based on this form.

Moving meditation

At its inception, when tai chi was practiced as a martial art, calming the mind and emptying it of all thought helped the practitioner to be able to respond swiftly and instinctively to an attack. Today, tai chi is primarily practiced for health reasons, and the slow graceful movement lends itself to the practice of meditation. Rather than being lost in thought, the practitioner calms his or her mind by focusing on the breath or the movements themselves. Over time, the mind develops the habit of becoming quiet during the practice of the form. When beginning the form, meditative visualizations can be used to enhance the flow of *chi* throughout the body. In the 1970s a master of tai chi, Cheng Man-Ch'ing, was asked whether he did seated meditation. He answered that tai chi was all the meditation he needed. You might find that the same applies to you.

 Work with this exercise now Turn to Exercise 22: Tai Chi Meditation on page 198 and follow the instructions.

Tai chi meditation

1 Stand with your feet together, and arms hanging at your sides.

2 Place your left foot apart from your right foot.

3 Allow your arms to float upward to chest height.

4 Draw your elbows back, keeping your arms away from your sides.

5 Now lower your arms slowly and let your weight sink.

Chi kung as meditation

Chi kung (pronounced "Chee-GUNG") is an aspect of Chinese medicine that aims to enhance the flow of Chi by combining meditation with movement and regulation of breathing. In ancient Chinese texts, *chi* is understood as the vital element that generates and unifies the universe. It is the energy that pervades all reality. Chi is produced by the interaction of *yin* and *yang*, the two opposite forces of the universe. It is often translated as "energy," "vital energy," "breath," or "vital breath." The word *kung* means work or technique. Chi kung, then, means "energy cultivation."

Chi kung is a health practice with strong meditative and metaphysical aspects designed to nourish and enhance the *chi* energy we receive from our parents at birth, and help us tap into the fundamental *chi* of the universe. Chi kung directly works with *chi* in order to integrate body, mind, and spirit. Some chi kung exercises help increase the store of *chi*, others help you move and circulate it using your mind and meditative techniques. By working with *chi*, chi kung can help

you prevent and heal from illness and develop a spiritual relationship with nature and the Universe.

Chi kung makes use of the meridian system of Chinese medicine—the pathways of energy channels by which *chi* flows through the body—and combines it with the meditative power of focused intention. The gentle movements of chi kung slowly build strength and vitality and enhance your immune system. By combining physical and breathing exercises with visualization and focused intent, chi kung becomes a powerful practice for mental, physical, and spiritual development.

Chi kung through the ages

References to *chi* are found as far back as 1800 BCE. The earliest references to chi kung are found in Taoist books from the Tang Dynasty (618-905) which describe breathing, visualization, or meditation techniques intended to help the practitioner achieve immortality. The exercises were also practiced to enhance health and balance body and mind, and were developed,

Chi kung meditation

refined and passed down over the centuries from teacher to disciple in strict confidence. Now this secret meditative knowledge is available to anyone who joins a class or buys a book on the subject.

Chi kung as spiritual practice

As chi kung practices became increasingly standardized, their spiritual or meditative aspects grew in importance. Chi kung was practiced in Taoist, Buddhist, and Confucian monasteries for health and spiritual development, and as a form of training in *chi* for the martial arts. In ancient times, the Zen Buddhist monks at Shaolin Temple in China practiced chi kung and meditation alongside the martial arts for which they are famed. They learned to cultivate their *chi* through the chi kung and their mind and spirit through the meditation. The practical health benefits of the exercises also kept the monks free of illness and allowed them to recover easily from injuries. As they unblocked and moved their chi with the exercises, they moved toward higher states of consciousness. For Chinese spiritual masters, the cultivation of body and mind alike were necessary to enlightenment.

 Work with this exercise now Turn to Exercise 23: Chi Kung Healing Meditation on page 202. After reading the instructions, practice the movement a few times, then proceed with the meditation.

 I'm not there yet If you have difficulty bending your knees or rising onto your toes, simply do the arm movements while standing with your feet flat on the floor.

Yoga as meditation

Today, most of us know yoga as a health practice from ancient India that involves holding and moving through various postures or *asanas*. The physical benefits of yoga practice are almost too numerous to mention. A short list includes improved joint function and digestion, enhanced flexibility and cardiovascular fitness, better posture and spinal health, and stress reduction and hormonal balance. Although the physical benefits of *asana* practice alone are extraordinary, in ancient India yoga was practiced within the context of a spiritual path. The *asanas* enhanced meditation and encouraged spiritual realization. In ancient India, the body and the mind were one.

The eight limbs of yoga

The most ancient text on the philosophy of Yoga, is the *Yoga Sutras of Patanjali* dating from the first century BCE. In this, we learn that yoga has eight aspects or "limbs" that together form a complete path. Following the eight limbs of classical yoga leads a yogi along a beautiful and inspiring path of physical and spiritual development.

The eight limbs in Sanskrit, the sacred language of India, are:

1 *Yama* moral behavior toward others
2 *Niyama* moral behavior toward oneself
3 *Asana* physical postures
4 *Pranayama* breath-control exercises
5 *Pratyahara* withdrawing the senses to still the mind
6 *Dharana* meditation for focus and concentration
7 *Dhyana* meditation for expanding mindfulness
8 *Samadhi* meditation that brings enlightenment.

The yogic path to your innermost self

The eight limbed path of classical yoga acknowledges that human beings are made up of five layers or koshas. The five layers progress from outer to inner. The innermost layer is the self, or *atman*, known as the eternal center of consciousness, or Absolute Reality, which is said to have never been born and will never die. Yoga as a spiritual and meditative practice encourages movement from our outermost layers to our most subtle interior core.

The *annamaya kosha* is the physical outer layer composed of skin, muscle tissue, bones, and organs. Meditation on awareness of the physical body deepens our overall awareness of life moment to moment.

Moving inward, the next layer is *pranamaya kosha*, the energy layer that involves the circulation of breath and prama life-energy. Meditation focused on awareness of the breath is an excellent choice for working with this layer.

Child Pose

Mana means "mind," and the *manomaya kosha* is the mental layer and the one associated with the nervous system; it is here that we process thoughts and emotions. Meditations that calm the mind and help us become aware of thoughts and emotions work on the *manomaya kosha*.

Moving toward the center, the next layer *vijanamaya kosha* is concerned with wisdom and higher states of consciousness. Meditations for this layer focus on the expansion of consciousness beyond thinking and our ordinary perception of reality.

The last and innermost layer before the self or *atman* is *anandamaya kosha*, also known as the body of bliss. This is the experience of joy and love beyond what thought can comprehend, or words can describe, and unrelated to any reason, cause, or willful action on your part. You simply rest in bliss. At the center, the realization of the self is the indescribable experience of enlightenment, the goal of yoga meditation.

 Work with this exercise now Turn to Exercise 24: Yoga Meditation on page 206. After reading the instructions, practice sitting on your heels a few times, then proceed with the full posture and meditation to experience the spiritual potential of yoga.

 ➤ **I'm not there yet** Use the cushions as directed to ease the stretch in your hips and back if necessary.

EXERCISES IN MOVEMENT MEDITATION

Meditation does not have to always involve sitting on a cushion. Movement meditation appeals to people who like to achieve a meditative state of mind by moving their bodies. The following exercises will give you a taste of various forms of movement meditation.

Meditative walking

Before you start this meditation, clear a path in your home so that you can walk without having to stop and move furniture or other obstacles. One option would be to walk down a long hallway and back. You can also practice walking meditation in your backyard or on a secluded walking path in a park.

Exercise 21 WALKING MEDITATION

 **Illustration** See pages 19–28 for illustrations showing sitting positions.

 **When to do this exercise** Practice walking meditation any time you care to do it. Once you are tuned in to meditative walking, you do not need always to start by sitting.

- **Sit down and practice** the Basic Breath Meditation (see page 66) for five minutes or so. When you feel your mind has settled, carefully stand up without disturbing your sense of calmness.

- **Once you are standing** make a fist with your left hand, tucking the thumb inside your fist. Position your fist in the center of the chest, at the level of your heart. Place your right palm on top of the fist and let your fingers wrap around it. Extend your elbows at the same height as the fist, keeping your forearms parallel to the floor.

- **Half-close your eyes** and relax them. Begin to walk around the room very slowly. Take a short half-step with each inhalation and exhalation. Keep following your breath.

- **As you continue to walk** focus on the complexity of this simple movement. Watch how your weight transfers from leg to leg, and rolls from the heel to the ball of the foot; observe how pushing off with your toes propels you forward; notice how you balance momentarily and think about the center of your balance below your navel.

- **Don't think about the movement** too much; just experience it. As you walk breathe into your belly, stay relaxed, and let your thoughts and your mind calm down.

- **Continue in this way** for 20 minutes or longer if you desire. When you are ready to end the session, come to a stop and bow slightly to mark the end of your practice.

My walking meditation experience

Questions to consider
How did I feel before the walking meditation?
How did I feel after the walking meditation?

Date _____ Time _____

_____

_____

_____

_____

_____

_____

_____

Date _____ Time _____

_____

_____

_____

_____

_____

_____

_____

Date _____ Time _____

_____

_____

_____

_____

_____

_____

_____

_____

Date _____ Time _____

_____

_____

_____

_____

_____

_____

_____

_____

_____

Exploring tai chi

As you practice the opening move of this Short Yang Style Form, consider it as a moment full of possibilities—like every other moment in your life. Think about how, unless you empty your mind of its constant thinking and strategizing and are fully present in the moment, you miss the many opportunities every moment has for growth and change. Before you start, find a quiet place to practice, preferably outdoors in a beautiful natural setting. You will need to wear loose comfortable clothing and flat shoes or work barefoot.

 Exercise 22 TAI CHI MEDITATION
CD REFERENCE TRACK 1 OR TRACK 6 (OPTIONAL)

 Illustration Step-by-step photographs of the movements are shown on page 185.

 When to do this exercise Practice tai chi any time you care to do it. The opening move of the Short Yang Style Form is a great antidote to stress.

- **Stand with your feet together,** toes slightly pointing out, arms hanging loosely at your sides. Stand quietly and take a moment to focus on your breath. Scan your body and notice how you feel. Notice any areas of tension and breathe into them. Now relax your shoulders and tuck in the base of your spine. Visualize your spine suspended from above by a golden thread.

- **Sink your weight into your right foot** and raise your left foot, placing it about shoulder-width from your right foot. Adjust your right foot so that both feet are parallel and facing forward. Make sure your weight is evenly distributed between both feet. Make a space under your arms as if you have a large egg beneath each armpit.

- **As you breathe in**, keep your arms, wrists, and fingers relaxed and allow your arms to float upward to chest height. Make sure your forearms are parallel to the ground and your shoulders are relaxed and still. Visualize *chi* being drawn up from the earth through points on the bottom and center of your feet, just below the ball; here, yin earth energy enters the body. Visualize your entire body being nourished by the energy of the earth. As you breathe out, slowly raise and straighten your fingers so that the tips face forward. Keep your wrists relaxed and slightly dropped.

- **Draw your elbows back** while keeping your arms slightly away from your sides. Try not to create tension in your back and shoulder blades.

- **Now lower your arms slowly** to your sides and let your weight sink. Relax your shoulders, hands, and fingers and allow your knees to bend slightly. Imagine roots extending down into the ground from your feet, and the golden thread attached to the top of your head pulling you into the sky. Continue to focus on your breath, feeling it as *chi* circulating throughout your body.

- **Practice this sequence three times** then stand quietly and meditate on your breath for a few minutes before closing your meditation.

My tai chi meditation experience

Question to consider
Was I able to feel *chi* energy moving through my body?

Date _____ **Time** _____

_____

_____

_____

_____

_____

_____

Date _____ **Time** _____

_____

_____

_____

_____

_____

_____

_____

Date _____ Time _____

_____

_____

_____

_____

_____

_____

_____

_____

Date _____ Time _____

_____

_____

_____

_____

_____

_____

_____

_____

Healing with chi kung

Reaching for the Sky is the first of the Eight Pieces of Silk Brocade, an elegant set of eight chi kung exercises first described in an 8th-century Chinese text. In this Taoist treatise, the Eight Brocades are attributed to one of the eight immortals of Chinese folklore and were developed to guarantee a long life.

They work by strengthening and encouraging the free flow of *chi*, toning organ systems, and clearing the mind of delusions or negativity. Find a quiet place to practice outdoors near mature trees. You will need to wear loose comfortable clothing and flat shoes or work barefoot.

Exercise 23 CHI KUNG HEALING MEDITATION

 Illustration Step-by-step photographs of the movements are shown on page 187.

 When to do this exercise Practice this healing meditation as often as you can. If you are trying to heal your body, do it every day.

- **Stand with your feet** shoulder-width apart and parallel to each other; let your arms hang loosely at your sides. Keep your knees unlocked and very slightly bent and your shoulders relaxed. Imagine that your whole body is suspended from a string at the top of your head. Close your eyes and take three belly breaths. Then stand for a few minutes and breathe normally to calm your mind.

- **Open your eyes and look forward.** Interlace your fingers, palms facing downward and slowly raise your arms in a circle above your head. Inhale as you stretch upward and at the same time, bend your knees slightly and rise up on your toes. As you breathe in, imagine golden light entering your body through your nose, clearing any problems you have with your breathing, your digestion or elimination.

- **As you exhale lower your heels** and let your feet rest flat on the floor as you lower your arms. Breathing out, visualize any illness or imbalance leaving your body as gray smoke.

- **Rest for a moment,** then inhale and stretch upward again, but this time with your palms facing toward the sky. As you inhale, imagine luminous white light entering your body through your nose and purifying any emotional problems you may be having, such as depression, anxiety, or fear. As you breathe out and lower your heels and arms, visualize your emotional difficulties leaving your body as gray smoke.

- **Repeat this set of movements** and accompanying visualizations nine times, alternating the direction in which your palms face. Then close your meditation.

My chi kung healing meditation experience

Questions to consider

Was I able to feel light and energy moving through my body?

Has practicing this exercise over time improved my health, energy, or mood?

Date _____ Time _____

_____

_____

_____

_____

_____

_____

_____

Date _____ Time _____

_____

_____

_____

_____

_____

_____

_____

Date _____ Time _____

_____

_____

_____

_____

_____

_____

_____

_____

Date _____ Time _____

_____

_____

_____

_____

_____

_____

_____

_____

Exploring yoga

Balasana, or Child Pose, is a very simple and extremely relaxing posture that, when combined with meditation, can help you experience the spiritual potential of yoga practice. Find a quiet, warm place to practice indoors; it is best to work on a yoga mat or folded blanket, and you may need a few thin cushions to make you comfortable if your legs or hips are stiff. You will need to wear loose clothing and remove your shoes, belt, watch, and jewelry.

Exercise 24 YOGA MEDITATION

 **Illustration** A photograph of the posture is shown on page 191.

 **When to do this exercise** Any yoga pose can be done at any time to help revitalize your health, strengthen your immune system, and further your spiritual practice.

- **Kneel on the mat or blanket,** resting your buttocks on your heels. If your buttocks don't comfortably reach your heels, place a cushion between your heels and buttocks. If your feet are uncomfortable, position a folded blanket or thin cushion here too. Rest your palms on your thighs.

- **Sit tall—imagine your spine** and head are suspended from a string—and as you exhale let your weight drop down through your buttocks and heels. Sit here, focusing on your out-breaths until your pelvis feels heavy and glued to your heels.

Keeping your weight on your heels, creep your hands forward, maintaining length at the front of your body. With each inhalation, lengthen the front of your torso slightly, and with each exhalation extend forward a little more. Let this forward movement gradually lower your chest until it rests on your thighs (or on a cushion). Rest your forehead on the floor (or on another cushion). Relax your arms by your sides, palms facing up beside your feet.

- **Now close your eyes** and reflect on the vastness of your inner landscape, from where your dreams, memories, and intuition emerge. Know that this inner realm is the most important aspect of who you are as a person. It is where you connect with your higher self, or higher power.

- **Begin to focus on your breath**, relax, and with each inhalation feel this vast expanse grow within you until it fills the universe itself. Generate a feeling of love and compassion for the entire endless universe and everyone in it—especially for yourself. Rest in that feeling of expansive love and caring.

- **When you are ready**, begin to gather your consciousness back from the universe to yourself as you are in Child Pose. Release your arms and gradually push yourself up on an inhalation, returning to your beginning kneeling position.

My yoga meditation experience

Questions to consider
Could I feel a sense of the universe while in this introspective pose?
How has this yoga meditation changed my experience of yoga?

Date _____ Time _____

_____

_____

_____

_____

_____

_____

_____

Date _____ Time _____

_____

_____

_____

_____

_____

_____

_____

MEDITATIONS FOR OPENING THE HEART

Meditation to foster loving-kindness

We all want to be loving and kind, but often find it difficult to put that aspiration into practice in daily life. The missing key may be forgetting that loving-kindness has to start with being loving and kind to ourselves. When Eastern Buddhist teachers came to the West to teach in the 1970s, they discovered a widespread tendency for Westerners to be hard on themselves. They found a lot of self-criticism, self-loathing, and feelings of inadequacy. In general, they found Westerners to have a low opinion of themselves, which translates into a problem with self-love. The traditional Buddhist teachings, instead of being inspiring and uplifting, would leave people feeling bad because they had a problem with self-hatred, and would turn whatever they heard against themselves. For example, a student hearing the teachings on unconditional love would feel inadequate because he or she had difficulty putting those teachings into practice. Rather than taking the teachings as inspiration, they were taken as judgment and criticism.

An antidote to those feelings is to begin to love oneself and treat oneself with patience and kindness. From that place grows the ability to love others.

Loving yourself is not narcissism

Loving yourself is not to be confused with self-indulgence or narcissism. On the other hand, making friends with yourself is not the same as giving in to every whim or refusing to work with bad habits. You may have explored spiritual teachings in a search for comfort and affirmation and relief from the realities and stresses of life. You may have longed to be healed and have your problems magically "fixed." When you started meditating, you may have found the unacceptable aspects of yourself came in conflict with your ideal of yourself as a spiritual person, and wished they would simply disappear. But authentic spiritual practice and meditation are about opening to life and to yourself completely and unconditionally—the good, the bad, and the ugly, the hurt, the wanting, the pain, and the joy.

Loving yourself is not about deciding who you think you should be and then spending the rest of your life trying to become that person. Nor is it about trying to be the ideal person your parents, your spouse, your boss, or anyone else in your life wants you to be. This is the opposite of self-love and a sure way to alienate yourself from yourself.

It takes a great deal of courage to love yourself and to relate to yourself directly as you are. It is easy to avoid looking at, or make excuses for, anger, moments of pettiness, seemingly voracious desires, or a sense of inadequacy and difficulty loving others. But these are the moments that offer you an opportunity to learn what self-love really is. Before you can work with yourself you have to acknowledge clearly where you are in life, and love yourself completely. From that background of love and compassion for yourself as you really are, you can move your life in a positive direction. You can begin to show real love to others because you now know how to love yourself. You can become truly capable of loving others as they are, rather than how you want them to be.

 Work with this exercise now Turn to Exercise 25: Meditation on Loving Myself on page 226 and follow the instructions.

Meditation to increase compassion

Compassion is the desire to relieve suffering. This desire can extend to yourself or to other sentient beings. One of the best ways to begin to work with compassion is to remember a time when you were awakened to feelings of compassion. Perhaps when someone in your family was ill and you wanted them to be relieved of their suffering, or when you saw on television the aftermath of an event that caused suffering, such as 9/11 or Hurricane Katrina or an earthquake.

Sometimes you just want people to be released from a difficult situation. You want them rescued from the rubble and brought to safety. But mostly things are not so simple. For example, it is not within your power to remove cancer from a loved one or get back the job you lost. So then you have to think about the source of suffering. If someone is seriously ill, of course you want him or her to be free of pain and to get better. But what you want on a deeper level is for him or her to be free

of the fear and mental suffering that can accompany serious illness. Likewise, if you lose your job you want to be free of the resentment and anxiety you may be feeling.

The problem with suffering is not that bad things happen—because they do and they always will. Rather, it is how we make suffering worse by our reactions to it. What we really wish for ourselves—and anyone else going through a painful situation—is to be free of the ongoing fear, bitterness, or depression related to that situation.

There is nothing wrong with emotion in any life event. But what we do with that emotion is the key to relieving suffering. We can make matters worse by continually reliving resentment, bitterness, anger, blame, fear, and depression. Or we can, by caring, move through these emotions and become free of the self-imposed suffering we create with our minds.

Tonglen meditation

Tibetan Buddhists have a special meditation for generating compassion and relieving suffering in themselves and others called tonglen. In the Tibetan language *tong* means "sending out" or "letting go" and *len* means "receiving" or "accepting."

In the practice of tonglen you mentally send or give away relief from suffering in the form of happiness, pleasure, or anything that feels good with your out-breath. As you breathe in, you inhale your own suffering or the suffering of others. This, of course, sounds a little scary. You may feel terrible at the thought of breathing in suffering and negativity and at the same time breathing out whatever good feelings you have. But once you give this a try, you realize that you have more goodness and compassion to give

and the courage to face more suffering than you ever knew. Tonglen meditation helps you to discover that you can be more open to others and to life, and be less possessive and territorial. You can give away your goodness and take on your own suffering and the suffering of others—and in the process become a more compassionate human being. Tonglen is not magic. You do not do this meditation expecting your own or others' suffering to go away. The point of tonglen meditation is simply to open your heart and mind.

Practicing tonglen

How do you practice tonglen meditation? First you breathe in your own suffering and then breathe out compassion for yourself. Start by thinking about a place in which you feel emotionally stuck or with ways in which you increase your own suffering.

Maybe you have an addiction or feel consumed with jealousy, anxiety, or fear. Work with that for a while—for however long it takes—until you feel some shift in your feelings toward yourself.

Then begin to work on behalf of those who are close to you: your parents, friends, and partner. Breathe in their suffering and give away your happiness to them on your out-breath. Next, practice giving and taking with those you may not know, perhaps someone in the news, who has suffered great harm or loss, an injured animal or a homeless person living in a shelter. Then, saving the best for last, work with those you consider your enemies, who you feel have hurt you. Then you begin to understand that, just like you, others suffer, and, just like you, they want to be happy; in that way you are alike.

Work with this exercise now Turn to Exercise 26: Tonglen Meditation on page 230 and follow the instructions.

➤ **I'm not there yet** If tonglen feels too difficult or if you are afraid of taking in the suffering of others, simply work with your own suffering. Once you feel comfortable generating compassion for yourself, try extending it to others.

Learning to rejoice

You begin this practice by learning to rejoice in your own good fortune, expressing gratitude for all that you have and all you have been given. This can be the smallest thing: the fact that the mail is delivered on time every day or that the daffodils are blooming. Many of us miss the good things in life because it is so easy to take them for granted. You most likely have a comfortable home, running water, and electricity—luxuries in many parts of the world. It may not be the home you dream of, but you have one, and this is something to celebrate.

Take care of the things you are fortunate to own and rejoice in the fact that you have them. When you reach for the pots and pans in your kitchen to prepare dinner, for example, thank them for their service in helping you feed yourself, friends, and family, and make sure you keep them in good shape. By doing this you will find yourself to be less dissatisfied in general and happier with what you do have. Everything around you has the power to inspire and uplift you if you let it, even your parched plant valiantly and loyally standing tall despite your neglect. Letting go of complaining about what is wrong and focusing on the joyful aspects of your surroundings will change your life.

Rejoicing in others' good fortune

Another aspect of this practice involves thinking about loved ones and rejoicing in their happiness, too. If your spouse got an excellent review at work, be glad that he or she is happy with the achievement. Rejoice when your child recovers from a cold. Finding and expressing joy in a loved one's good fortune is fairly easy to do. It is a little more difficult to appreciate the good fortune of those less close to you. In these relationships you may struggle with competitive and jealous feelings. You may feel a twinge of envy if a work colleague or friend from your student days does well in life. If your best friend finds a handsome, caring boyfriend and you have not been so successful in love, you may feel unable to rejoice. But when this happens, take a moment to contemplate this fact: when you close down your heart in any way it diminishes your own joy.

Work with this exercise now Turn to Exercise 27: Meditation on Rejoicing on page 234 and follow the instructions.

➤ **I'm not there yet** Being able to rejoice for other people's lives may not happen right away, but try not to give up on yourself or the practice. Have confidence that, with practice, you will be able to open your heart and celebrate others' good fortune.

Living with equanimity

You have learned as you have worked through the meditations in this book that you have a tendency to sort people and experiences into three baskets: attraction, aversion, and neutral. This is the normal way of looking at the world. But how do you begin to see the world differently—with equanimity?

Dislike is not a bad emotion in itself. Disliking a situation, feeling uncomfortable and wanting to get away from it can save you from harm. For example, if you are walking home alone at night, you may feel afraid as you look down a dark street you need to go down. Acting on that feeling of aversion, you call a friend and get a ride instead.

In the same way, desire is not bad in itself, either. An initial desire for someone may lead you to marry, have children, and grow old with a lovely and loving companion. Working with equanimity is not about becoming Dr. Spock in "Star Trek," who lives without emotion or feelings of preference for any thing, person, or situation. Living with equanimity is not about giving up your passion for life; rather, it is about deepening your ability to love unconditionally.

Making the effort

It takes effort to make equanimity part of your life. It starts by having basic respect and concern for every person on earth, regardless of how you feel about them. Then you begin to work on the three attitudes of attachment, aversion, and indifference more directly. For example, to overcome possessive attachment for someone, meditate on impermanence, recalling that everything and everyone changes, and nothing lasts. One day, death will separate you from that person. Or you will separate for other reasons. The more attached you are, the more pain you will suffer when separation comes. Therefore it is wise to begin to distinguish possessive attachment from love. Practicing unconditional love will deepen and strengthen your relationship and help you when the inevitable happens.

To overcome uncaring indifference toward strangers—those who are neither friends nor enemies—begin to think about the kindness of strangers and the countless ways you depend on them. You could think, "Without this grocery worker stocking the shelves, I would have no food to buy. Without this bus driver I would have no way to get to work."

To overcome anger and aversion toward someone who has hurt you, begin by reflecting on why they harmed you. You can consider whether you contributed to the situation in any way. Or you can ask yourself if this person is under the control of their delusions, which caused him or her to harm you. Then you can review your own problems and delusions. By doing this you see that the other person and you

are alike. You are both suffering in your own way and it is suffering that causes all of us to harm ourselves and others. Thinking this way, even if you continue to find it difficult to be with this person, can begin to cool your anger and generate compassion and acceptance.

 Work with this exercise now Turn to Exercise 28: Meditation on Equanimity on page 238 and follow the instructions.

EXERCISES TO OPEN THE HEART

The following exercises are based on Buddhist teachings called the Four Immeasurables, though you do not have to be a Buddhist to either practice or benefit from them. These four exercises work together synergistically to help open the heart and increase your ability to love unconditionally.

Meditation on loving-kindness

This exercise puts you in touch with your higher self: that part of you that, whether you know it or not, is always there—the quiet, knowing, nonjudging, loving, wise observer. For the purposes of this exercise, think of that person as your parent aspect and think of your ordinary self as your child aspect.

 Exercise 25 MEDITATION ON LOVING MYSELF
CD REFERENCE TRACK 1 OR TRACK 6 (OPTIONAL)

 Illustration See pages 19–28 for illustrations showing sitting positions.

 When to do this exercise Practice loving-kindness when you are being particularly hard on yourself for something you feel you have done, or failed to do.

- **Choose a sitting meditation posture** that you find comfortable (see page 42). Start by focusing on your breath for a few minutes to settle your body and mind.

- **Now begin to observe** the child self within you, and notice your thoughts and emotions, how your body feels, and any sense of shame or guilt you may be feeling about something you have done or failed to do. Take time just to sit with any uncomfortable feelings or disappointments you may have about yourself. Feel fully any feelings of being unlovable, damaged, or unworthy.

- **Now switch your focus** to the parent aspect of your inner self. From the mind of an enlightened and loving parent, see that suffering child within; the part of you that feels negative toward yourself, as perfect and lovable as you are.

- **Accept your child as he or she is.** Accept him or her completely and unconditionally. Feel yourself as a loving parent and let your heart overflow with love and caring for the child in you that feels so badly about himself or herself. Look at your inner child with compassion for the ways in which he or she suffers. Look at him or her with affection and love, seeing clearly the wonderful strengths and positive qualities as well as the various weaknesses. Open your heart and embrace your child with complete, unconditional love as he or she is right now at this moment in time.

- **Now merge the parent and child** aspects of yourself back into one person. Sit for a moment basking in the feeling of unconditional love and acceptance for every part of yourself.

My loving myself experience

Questions to consider
How did it feel to be a parent to my inner child?
Has this meditation helped relieve any feelings of self-criticism or self-hatred
I may have been experiencing?

Date _____ Time _____

_____

_____

_____

_____

_____

_____

_____

Date _____ Time _____

_____

_____

_____

_____

_____

_____

_____

Date _____ **Time** _____

_____

_____

_____

_____

_____

_____

_____

_____

Date _____ **Time** _____

_____

_____

_____

_____

_____

_____

_____

_____

Meditation to relieve suffering

In the beginning you may find this practice quite difficult, but if you stay at it over time your compassion will grow and flourish. If you feel blocked or any resistance when practicing, just generate compassion for your feeling of being closed off. Simply acknowledging your "closedness" can be transformative. Everything can be worked with in this practice—nothing is left out.

 ## Exercise 26 TONGLEN MEDITATION
CD REFERENCE TRACK 1 OR TRACK 6 (OPTIONAL)

 Illustration See pages 19—28 for illustrations showing sitting positions.

 When to do this exercise When you wish to relieve your own suffering and open your heart to the suffering of others. Tonglen meditation can be done at any time, either in a formal meditation session or at the moment you experience your own or someone else's suffering.

- **If sitting to meditate**, choose a sitting meditation posture that you find comfortable (see page 42) in a warm, quiet place. Meditate on your breath for a few minutes to clear your mind.

- **Let go of the focus on your breath** and let your mind rest for a few minutes in a state of openness and stillness. Feel your mind as spacious, clear, and lucid.

- **Now return your focus to** your breath, but this time visualize breathing in a sensation of heat, darkness, and heaviness so that you feel somewhat uncomfortable. Then breathe out a feeling of coolness, brightness, and light so that you experience a sense of openness and freshness.

- **Now choose a painful personal experience** or situation. For instance if you are feeling unhappy in your job or your marriage say to yourself, "May I be free from suffering and the root of suffering." Then breathe in that pain for yourself and everyone else experiencing that feeling. Breathe out your compassion in the form of confidence and self-acceptance for yourself and everyone else suffering from feelings of inadequacy. Breathe in and out this way for a few minutes.

- **Now practice tonglen** for someone you love, saying, "May he/she be free from suffering and the root of suffering" and breathing in their pain and the pain of everyone who is in the same situation as your loved one. If your loved one is seriously ill, for example, include not just him or her in your thoughts, but everyone else suffering from that illness. Breathe out your compassion in the same way.

- **Now try repeating the practice** for people you consider to be your enemies— those who have hurt you or hurt others. Think of those enemies as having the same confusion and pain as you do. Breathe in their pain and send them relief.

- **End your meditation** by focusing on your breath for a few minutes.

My tonglen meditation experience

Questions to consider
Was this meditation difficult for me?
How did I feel after practicing tonglen for myself?
How did I feel after practicing tonglen for others?

Date _____ Time _____

_____

_____

_____

_____

_____

_____

_____

Date _____ Time _____

_____

_____

_____

_____

_____

_____

_____

Date _____ Time _____

_____

_____

_____

_____

_____

_____

_____

_____

_____

_____

Date _____ Time _____

_____

_____

_____

_____

_____

_____

_____

_____

_____

_____

Connecting with joy

It takes effort to slow down and take in all the small joyful details of your life—those things you often take for granted—and you will need real courage to work with negative feelings about other's good fortune, such as competition or jealousy. This meditation on rejoicing will help you to connect better with your own joy and good fortune and that of others—this is the key to happiness.

 ## Exercise 27 MEDITATION ON REJOICING
CD REFERENCE TRACK 1 OR TRACK 6 (OPTIONAL)

 Illustration See pages 19—28 for illustrations showing sitting positions.

 When to do this exercise Rejoicing can be done at any time, either in a formal meditation session or at any moment when you wish to take pleasure in life.

- **If you are sitting to meditate**, choose a sitting posture that you find comfortable (see page 42). Begin by taking three deep belly breaths, then meditate on your breath for a few minutes. When you feel calm and relaxed begin following the steps.

- **Bring to mind five objects, situations,** or people you are grateful to have in your life. These should be easy to think of. Spend some time focusing on each example and generating a genuine feeling of gratitude.

- **Now think of something** that has happened to your partner, spouse, or another close loved one that made you happy. Recall that event and relive the feelings of joy and gratitude you felt at the time.

- **Now bring to mind** a positive event or situation in the life of a friend or acquaintance that gave you mixed feelings. For example, when a co-worker got a rise and promotion, a friend made big money from a business venture, or your neighbor's child won a national competition. Bring to mind any pangs of jealousy you may have felt. Then stretch your heart a bit and try to feel real joy for their good fortune. Simply give away your joy without feeling diminished in any way yourself. Notice how much better this feels than harboring feelings of jealousy.

- **Sit for a few minutes** simply experiencing this feeling of joy for your friend. Remember that there is so much suffering in life and be happy that he or she has experienced a moment of happiness and joy.

- **End your meditation** when you are ready. Dedicate your meditation to your own joy and happiness and that of others.

My meditation on rejoicing experience

Questions to consider
Did this meditation expand my own feelings of joy?
Did this meditation increase my ability to rejoice in other people's happiness?

Date _____ Time _____

_____

_____

_____

_____

_____

_____

_____

Date _____ Time _____

_____

_____

_____

_____

_____

_____

_____

Date _____ Time _____

_____

_____

_____

_____

_____

_____

_____

_____

Date _____ Time _____

_____

_____

_____

_____

_____

_____

_____

_____

Working with unconditional love

This is one of the most challenging meditation techniques in the book, but once you start practicing it regularly you will find it to be one of the most rewarding. It will transform the way you react to difficult situations and change the way in which you interact with everyone on the planet for the better.

 ## Exercise 28 MEDITATION ON EQUANIMITY
CD REFERENCE TRACK 1 OR TRACK 6 (OPTIONAL)

 Illustration See pages 19–28 for illustrations showing sitting positions.

 When to do this exercise You can meditate on equanimity at any time, either in a formal meditation session or at any other moment of the day.

- **If sitting to meditate**, choose a sitting meditation posture that you find comfortable (see page 42). Begin by meditating on your breath for a few minutes to calm your mind and relax your body.

- **Now meditate for a moment** on the benefits of equanimity: think about how it allows you to be present with an open heart no matter how wonderful or difficult conditions are.

- **Since equanimity is grounded in the practice** of letting go, bring to mind any major changes or difficult situations in the past year. Perhaps you were made unemployed, changed roles, lost a loved one, or were diagnosed with a disease. Meditate on the fact that the nature of life is change and that you have very little control over much of what happens. Think about everything negative that happened over the past year and mentally let it go, releasing whatever happened back to the universe.

- **Bring to mind the objects**, people, and situations in life that make you happy. Feel your sense of attachment to them and your desire to cling to them. Imagine what it would be like to love the people in your life unconditionally, that is, whether they are with you and provide you with happiness and pleasure or not. Feel your heart open with unconditional love and release the people, objects, and situations that you are attached to back to the universe.

- **Now think about how you** interact with strangers. To overcome any uncaring indifference you may feel toward them, imagine a stranger on a bus. Think about how he or she tries to find happiness and to avoid suffering just like you. Think about how much you have in common. Feel for his or her pain and rejoice in his or her happiness.

- **Meditate on your breath** for a few minutes, and on the out-breath let go of any remaining attachment, aversion, or indifference you may be feeling before ending your practice.

My meditation on equanimity experience

Question to consider
In what ways can the practice of equanimity help me in my life?

Date _____ Time _____

_____

_____

_____

_____

_____

_____

_____

Date _____ Time _____

_____

_____

_____

_____

_____

_____

_____

INSPIRATIONS

You will find these meditations on the CD that accompanies this book. Use them as directed in the exercises, or let them inspire your own meditation practices.

CD TRACK 2
Body Scan

THIS TRACK HELPS YOU TO RELAX AND PREPARE FOR MEDITATION.

- **Lie on your back** on the floor with your feet slightly apart and your arms relaxed and slightly away from your body. Make sure you are completely comfortable, then close your eyes.

- **Feel your feet.** Sense their weight. Consciously relax them and let them sink into the floor. Start with relaxing your toes, then the ball of your foot, the arch, your heels, and your ankles.

- **Relax your lower legs.** Feel your knees. Sense their weight. Consciously relax them and feel any tension dissolve.

- **Relax your upper legs and thighs.** Feel their weight. Consciously relax them and feel them sink into the floor.

- **Now feel your abdomen and chest.** Sense your breathing. Imagine your abdomen and chest completely relax. Deepen your breathing slightly and feel your abdomen and chest completely relaxed.

- **Feel your buttocks.** Sense their weight. Consciously relax them and feel them sink into the floor.

- **Feel your hands.** Sense their weight. Consciously relax them and feel them sink into the floor.

- **Feel your upper arms.** Sense their weight. Consciously relax them and feel them sink into the floor.

- **Feel your shoulders**. Sense their weight. Consciously relax them and release any tense areas.

- **Feel your neck**. Sense its weight. Consciously relax it and feel it sink into the floor.

- **Now feel your head and skull**. Sense its weight. Consciously relax it and let the floor support your head.

- **Pay attention to your mouth and jaw**. Consciously relax them. Pay particular attention to your jaw muscles and unclench them if you need to. Feel your mouth and jaw relax.

- **Feel your eyes**. Sense if there is tension in your eyes. Relax your eyelids and feel the tension slide off the eyes.

- **Feel your face and cheeks**. Consciously relax the muscles in your face and feel any tension release.

- **Mentally scan your body**. If you find any place that is still tense, then consciously relax that place and let the tension dissipate.

- **When you are ready** open your eyes and stretch.

Classic Seven-point Meditation Posture

THIS TRACK DETAILS HOW TO GET INTO A MORE ADVANCED SITTING POSITION FOR
MEDITATION, WHICH GIVES YOU A VERY STABLE BASE. START WITH BARE FEET.
NOTE AVOID THIS POSTURE IF YOU HAVE KNEE PROBLEMS.

- **Create a stable basis** for your posture. Sit on a thin cushion on the floor, barefoot, with your back straight. Take your right foot in your hands and slowly place it on your left thigh, as close to the crease of your hip as you can. Now, take your left foot in your hands and slowly place it on your right thigh, as close to the crease of your hip as possible.

- **Rest your hands in your lap** about four fingers' width below your navel. Your right hand is placed in the left hand, palms upwards, with the tips of the thumbs slightly raised and gently touching.

- **Allow a bit of space** between your upper arms and your torso. Make sure your shoulders are level and your chest is open and relaxed.

- **Keep your spine as straight as possible** without leaning backward, or slouching forward. Let the weight of your head fall evenly on your neck. Your head is tipped a little forward with the chin slightly tucked in so that your eyes are cast down.

- **Your mouth is relaxed** and your lips are very slightly parted. The tip of your tongue touches the back of your upper teeth.

- **Your eyes** are neither wide open nor completely closed but remain half open and gaze down along the line of the nose.

Basic Breath Meditation

THIS TRACK INTRODUCES THE KEY BREATHING TECHNIQUE USED IN ALL THE
MEDITATION EXERCISES IN THIS BOOK.

- **Take a deep in-breath** into your belly and slowly release. Repeat three times. Then, breathe normally, remembering to breathe into your belly. Release all your worries and cares as you exhale and simply be present in the moment.

- **As you breathe in and out**, focus on the sensation of the breath at your nostrils as it passes over your upper lip. Place your attention there, at the point of the incoming and outgoing breath. Once in a while, check to see that you are still breathing into your belly.

- **Keep your body as still as possible**, which will help still your mind. Try not to readjust your posture or fidget. Imagine you are a mountain: strong, calm, and stable.

- **When thoughts intrude**—and they will—just release them as you exhale. Try not to become emotionally involved with them. See them arise, pass through your mind, and disappear, like clouds moving across the sky. Simply return to focusing on your breath. Do not become discouraged if you have to do this over and over. Return to focus on your breath each time with gentleness and kindness.

- **Now turn off your CD player** and continue, on your own, to meditate for a minimum of 20 minutes.

Meditation on the Shri Yantra

THIS TRACK GUIDES YOU THROUGH THE YANTRA DIAGRAM ON PAGE 150.

- **First focus on the square periphery** of the Shri yantra and contemplate the obstacles to your spiritual development, such as worldly desire, anger, greed, or jealousy.

- **Next focus on the 16 petals** that represent the 16 aspects of your body and the world that keep you caught up in your own ego and prevent you from furthering your spiritual knowledge. They are the five elements (earth, water, fire, air, and space), the ten sense organs (the ears, skin, eyes, tongue, nose, mouth, feet, hands, arms, and genitals) and the dualistic mind.

- **Now move your attention inward**, to the ring of eight petals. These petals represent additional obstacles to spiritual development, such as negative speech, the tendency to grasp after things, and approaching everything in life with attachment, aversion, or indifference. Meditate on how these limitations affect your spiritual growth.

- **Now focus on the outer 14 triangles** that represent aspects of your subtle body. According to the Hindu tradition, your body has energy channels through which your vital energy flows. If you can't feel the channels, just acknowledge that you have them.

- **Moving inward, focus on the next ten triangles**. These represent various vital energies that flow through the channels of your body. Meditate on the fact that you are not just a physical being, but also an energetic being.

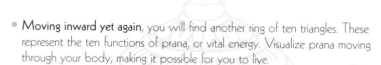

- **Moving inward yet again**, you will find another ring of ten triangles. These represent the ten functions of prana, or vital energy. Visualize prana moving through your body, making it possible for you to live.

- **The next ring is made up of eight triangles.** Three of them represent the three principles of nature according to the Hindu tradition: sattva, rajas, and tamas. Sattva is associated with purity, intelligence, and calmness of mind; rajas is the force behind creation, expressed as passion, egotism, and restlessness; and tamas equates with inertia, expressed as resistance to change. Meditate on these aspects of nature and how they manifest in your life.

- **You have now arrived at the innermost triangle.** Here, meditate on the fact that your normal understanding of the world is dualistic—you falsely perceive the separateness of subject and object, and of yourself from others.

- **You have arrived at the small dot,** the *bindu* at the center of the yantra, which symbolizes your innermost self. Now meditate on your self as whole and one with everything in the universe for several minutes before ending your meditation.

CD TRACK 8
Visualizing the Buddha

THIS TRACK GUIDES YOU THROUGH THE MEDITATION ON PAGES 170–171.

- **Sit quietly in the meditation posture** of your choice and allow your mind to become calm, letting the concerns of the day drop away. Imagine all your worries dissolving into the vast expanse of a clear blue sky that stretches into the distance as far as you can see. The blue sky symbolizes the pure, original nature of your mind unaffected by everyday thoughts, emotions, and projections.

- **After dwelling in this calm blue space** for a while, imagine a flat grassy plain in front of you with beautiful snow-capped mountain peaks in the distance. Notice the brilliance of the colors of the grass and mountains. Next, in the foreground notice a bodhi tree—the tree under which the Buddha achieved enlightenment. It has a silver trunk, broad branches, and dark green, heart-shaped leaves. Beneath the tree is a cushion covered with a pure white cloth.

- **On the white cloth appears** a large golden lotus flower and on that flower sits Shakyamuni Buddha, cross-legged in meditation. His body is made of luminous golden light and his hair is black and curly. He wears the yellow robes of a monk, his hands rest in his lap one on top of the other, and he is smiling serenely at you with his eyes half-closed. Surrounded by an aura of golden light, he radiates a feeling of deep peacefulness and compassion. Feel this warmth and compassion directed toward you.

- **Now visualize a ray of golden light** emanating from the heart of the Buddha and gently entering your own heart. Down this ray of light stream golden letters which also pour into your heart. They make up the mantra OM MUNI MUNI MAHA MUNAYE SOHA, the mantra of Shakyamuni Buddha. Visualize the golden ray of light and the mantra syllables healing any mental or physical illness that you may have.

- **While maintaining this visualization,** feel the Buddha's wisdom and compassion entering into you and transforming your heart and mind. Sit quietly and meditate on this image.

- **Now begin to dissolve the visualization** you have built up in your mind in reverse order until you are left again with the vast expanse of blue sky. Then let the blue sky also fade away as you bring your meditation to a close.

Index

Acknowledgments

Executive Editor Sandra Rigby
Senior Editor Lisa John
Senior Art Director Penny Stock
Designer Cobalt ID
Picture Researcher Marian Sumega
Assistant Production Controller Vera Janke

Picture credits

Alamy Fredrik Renander 219; Friedrich Stark 52; PhotoAlto 2; Sherab 215

Corbis Aaron Horowitz 181; Ale Ventura/PhotoAlto 10; Alison Wright 119; BSPI 117; Bettmann 121; Charles & Josette Lenars 123; Christophe Boisvieux 93; Lindsay Hebberd 115; moodboard 64; Studio DL 183; Werner Forman 153

Fotolia Bernd S 25; BibiDesign 16; Bruce Jones 63; Rido 51; sming 4; Svetlana Larina 216; Unclesam 1

Octopus Publishing Group 83, 84, 86, 91, 160, 212; Paul Bricknell 32, 59, 89, 94, 221, 223; Russell Sadur 9, 12, 20, 27, 185, 187, 191; Ruth Jenkinson 19, 23, 25, 28, 29, 57, 60, 128, 224

Photolibrary Antonello Lanzellotto 125; Nico Stengert 126; Nobuaki Sumida 157; Peter Frank 179; Robert Harding Travel 189; TAO Images Limited 147

Superstock Image Asset Management Ltd 211